I SHALL RAISE THEE UP
Ancient Principles for Lasting Greatness

Michael Holmes

I Shall Raise Thee Up
Ancient Principles for Lasting Greatness
by Michael Holmes

Printed in the United States of America

ISBN 978-1-60791-883-7

Dedicated to my family—my wife and son
who inspire
me to push for greatness everyday.

Acknowledgements

I think it was Steve Jobs who said, "It takes a lot of people to make a one-man show." I would have to agree with him. With that being said, I'd like to give thanks to those who helped me along the way, poured into me, corrected me, and helped pull the best out of me.

To my beautiful wife, Nathlin, thank you for your love, patience, character, and perseverance. You have been a constant source of encouragement and support. Thank you for being there; I can't imagine my life without you.

To my son Ethan whose bubbling personality makes me appreciate the fact that the simplest things are the most profound. I hope I can be as a good a father to you as you've been a son to me.

To my mother who raised me by herself since I was 13, thank you.

To Rev. Estelle Coye, thank you for your words of encouragement and wisdom. They mean more to me than you could ever imagine.

To the late Gloria "Aunty G" Gouldbourne, thank you for believing in me when others had given up. Your love and support I can never forget.

To Minister Tiffany Gordon, thank you for taking the time to review the book. Thank you for your thoughts, suggestions, and comments. Your knowledge, wisdom, and ability to right discern the Word of Truth have constantly kept me on my toes.

To Bro. Tony Brown, thank you also for believing in me. That belief gave me the courage to believe in myself; thank you for helping me to see what I was unable to.

To Bro. Patrick Francis, thank you for also believing in me. The earliest memories I have are you telling people, "I see something great in this young man." Well, it takes a great man to recognize "great" potential. Thank you.

To Rev. Lowell Spencer, thank you for encouraging me to "keep holding on." Thank you for wise advice, prudent direction, and a caring heart. I'm forever grateful.

To Elder Eldwin Rochford, thank you for your razor sharp knowledge of the Word, your devotion to your family, and your willingness to serve others—you have been a true example. I consider you a Paul in the faith—thank you for being a living epistle.

Contents

Paul said, *"Don't push your way to the front; don't sweet-talk your way to the top. Put yourself aside, and help others get ahead. Don't be obsessed with getting your own advantage. Forget yourselves long enough to lend a helping hand."* What does true greatness mean? Find out how to unlock the hidden greatness in you.

Principles are natural laws that are timeless, timely, and inflexible. Truly effective people learn and apply them in every area of their lives. Principles don't change and unlike a passing fad never go out of style. Find out why people who obey them reap rewards while those who don't reap consequences.

People who do great things and/or become great people tend not to fit in. How did a man like Barack Obama who was excluded from many circles come to be embraced by so many around the globe? Find out how isolation played its part in his ascension.

Desire must be present before any great work is done or great person is raised up. It is the starting point of all achievement. There has to be a burning desire for the realization of something as well as the belief it can be done. No great work was ever accomplished without desire.

Whatever you build will be built on the bedrock of your character. With God promotion is never the primary focus—the development of sound character is. Its one thing to attain something it's another thing to maintain it. Sound character helps maintain what you've attained.

The law that states every plan, achievement, or purpose must be seen before it can be realized. Why is it that a company or organization with a deeply entrenched long-term vision, seems to blow past competitors whose only ambition is to remain open? Why is that the leader who envisions what *can be* seems to go further and gain more influence than those who only see what *it is*? It's because the law of vision is at work constantly producing rewards for obedience and consequences for disobedience.

The law that states one must render more and better service than immediately paid for with a pleasing attitude. Kevin Liles was an unpaid intern at Def Jam who in nine years ascended the ranks to become its president. Vince Papale was a bouncer who became the NFL's oldest rookie and had his life filmed by Disney. What makes them similar? They both used the law of the extra mile.

1

INTRODUCTION

"...Even for this same purpose have I raised thee up, that I might shew My power in thee, and that My Name might be declared throughout all the earth." [1]

Raise up: *def.* change the arrangement or position of

Everyone desires to be great. Regardless of color, culture, profession, gender, and the like everyone desires to be better. One study found that in 2003 the total self improvement market (incl. revenues of weight loss products) was worth $8.56 billion; the bulk of the market share was in the **General Motivational/ Spiritual/ Self Help** segment with 55%; the closest contender was the **Weight Loss** segment with 15.1%. [2] But without the research and figures common sense testifies to the fact that within the human heart longs the desire to be better.

God raises up people. He is the Author of time. As the Author He has the right and responsibility to pick the characters, the plot, the climax, and the ending. He is the invisible Hand behind the drama of life; He cues the curtain and knows when to bring each character on and when to take them off. God is in control. *"For exaltation comes neither from the east nor from the west nor from the south. But God is the Judge: He puts down one, and exalts another."* [3]

Oddly enough the idea for this book came while I was riding the bus to a job that I hated. The trip was two hours long and so there was plenty of time to ponder and read. One day the concept of being raised up sprang into my mind. Prior to that I was replaying the events of my life up to that point and wondering how in the world I got into the mess I was in? Not only did I hate the job but it was just barely getting me by financially. With a wife and with a new son on the way, I was thinking, "There's **got** to be a way out of this."

So like any good idea it had to be nursed. I quickly took out pen and paper and jotted the idea down. When I reached my job I quickly emailed the publisher of a gospel magazine and told her I had an article. She said write it up and get it to her. I did and after a week emailed it to her. Within another week she emailed me back and told me what I wrote was too long and not current enough for the magazine (in hindsight she was right). So this failed article, birthed out of a brainstorm on a cold bus, headed to a job that I hated, is now a book and this book is now in your hands.

Wait a Minute…Is That Person Christian?

"For in Him we live, and move, and have our being; as certain also of your own poets have said, 'For we are also His offspring.'" [4]

The poet Paul is referring to is Aratus. He was of Greek origin and was admired in antiquity; in fact, the line he quotes is from the poet's work *Phaenomena.* [5] So when attempting to explain spiritual truths to the unsaved, Paul was skilled enough to use the works of the unsaved to bring the point home.

Throughout this book quotes and sayings from business leaders, philosophers, thought leaders, and etc will be used to validate points. Paul is my example of how to use the thoughts of "secular" people to drive home spiritual truths. Some may scoff saying, "How could secular quotes be used to explain Christian truths?" Well here are my answers:

1. **If it's God's truth then its relevance can extend beyond God's people.** Truths are applicable to the saint as well as the sinner. If both step off a cliff, both are subject to the laws of gravity, and both will fall regardless of relationship to God. God's truth is greater than any one person or people. The last time I checked He was still *"the God of all flesh."* [6]

2. **If it's God's truth it should be relevant always.** Truth is never created; it is only discovered and redis-covered. I make no claim of creating these truths. I could not. They existed before me and they'll exist after me. They were relevant then, are relevant now, and will forever be relevant. Truth will stand the test of time. *"A lie has a short life, but truth lives on forever."* [7]

How to Get the Most Out of This Book

"Dear friends, do you think you'll get anywhere in this if you learn all the right words but never do anything?" [8]

George Bernard Shaw once said, "If you teach a man anything, he will never learn." He was absolutely right. Learning is an active process not a passive one. We learn by doing. So the best ways to learn this book are:

- **Apply its lessons.** The book wasn't written just for learning but rather application; and it won't profit you if it's not applied. To read this book and not apply what was read is like *"a man who looks intently at his natural face in a mirror. For he looks at himself and goes away and at once forgets what he was like."* [9] The man sees what he can become, but after a while forgets about it, and remains who he is.
- **Teach its lessons.** Teach others what you have learned. There is an educational term called "teach back." This simply says that as you learn something you teach it back to others, and as you teach it to others you "learn back" what you taught. Share what you learned with somebody. Help them stir up the greatness they have in them. Group settings are one of the best ways to learn something. A group setting offers a melting pot of different experiences, points of view, and insight. No one person knows everything (I know I don't!). *"You use steel to sharpen steel, and one friend sharpens another."* [10] At the end of each chapter are questions to stimulate group discussion. Keep in mind: we grow together. Our lives are interrelated. I can never be all I'm supposed to be if you're not all you're supposed to be, and vice versa. To make people achieve their greatness is to become great, to help others find their voice is to find your own, and to give to someone is to give to yourself.

You Were Meant For Greatness

So in hindsight, I guess taking the bus to a job that I hated was a blessing in disguise. If I didn't there'd be no idea, if there was no idea there'd be no failed article, and if there was no failed article there'd be no book, and if there was no book we wouldn't be talking right now.

It's funny though, no matter how much I hear it I can never seem to get it through my thick skull: God is always blessing. I guess it never fully registers because when "bad" things come into my life I ask, "How can that be His blessing?" How can I be blessed and unemployed? Blessed and broke? Blessed and depressed? Or like Joseph, how can I be blessed and be in prison? Or like Moses, how can I be blessed on the backside of the desert? Or like David, how can I be blessed and be on the run from Saul? Or like Elijah, how can I be blessed under a juniper tree not wanting to live anymore? Or like John, be blessed when I'm isolated from everyone I know on the Island of Patmos? The answer is found in the concept of blessing: **a blessing speaks to the end of a thing**. Being blessed means that all minor afflictions are preparation for a greater end; blessings prepare us to become the person we need to be. The school of "hard knocks" teaches us lessons we wouldn't have learned otherwise. So, in that respect, we are all blessed.

Everything in your life up to this point has been preparing you towards a great end. Your path is *"as the shining light, that shineth more and more unto the perfect day."* [11] He's getting you ready...and deep down...you always knew that yourself. When God does raise you up, in hindsight **every-thing** will make sense, and in the end you'll be able to say to Him, *"My troubles turned out all for the best— they forced me to learn from Your Textbook."* [12]

2

WHAT IS GREATNESS

*"They started arguing over which of them would be
most famous. When Jesus realized how much this
mattered to them, He brought a child to His side.
'Whoever accepts this child as if the child were Me,
accepts Me,' He said. 'And whoever accepts Me,
accepts the One Who sent Me. You become great by
accepting, not asserting. Your spirit, not your size,
makes the difference.'" [1]*

**"Be not afraid of greatness; some are born great,
some achieve greatness, and others have greatness thrust upon them."**—William Shakespeare,
English poet and writer

The definition of greatness is as varied as the people who
use it. One definition may be to rule a nation while
another definition may be to be a good father, husband,
worker, and responsible citizen. Who's to say either is
wrong? But in spite of the different definitions there is one
thing that characterizes true greatness: service. **To serve is
to be great.** Paul when he talks about greatness and service
says, *"Don't push your way to the front; don't sweet-talk*

your way to the top. Put yourself aside, and help others get ahead. Don't be obsessed with getting your own advantage. Forget yourselves long enough to lend a helping hand." [2] It is that helping *"others get ahead"* mentality that births true greatness. True greatness is not becoming great at the expense of others but rather at the expense of self; finding ways to serve the needs of people **and make them better.** We were all meant to be great because we were all meant to serve.

Of course such greatness comes at the expense of personal sacrifice, but when the history books are written, it's these people that stand out among the anonymous. It's these people that become examples to us. **There is only one problem with greatness**—and that is when a person decides to live **beneath** their definition. There's something wrong with having a level five potential but living at a level one or two. You were meant to be great!

There's a song that really emphasizes, in my mind, what true greatness is:

"If I can help somebody as I travel along,
If I can cheer somebody with a word or song
If I can help somebody from doing wrong,
My living shall not be in vain.

If I can do my duty as a good man ought,
If I can bring back beauty to a world up wrought,
If I can spread love's message, as the Master taught,
Then my living shall not be in vain." [3]

Seeds of Greatness

The great God Who formed you placed in you seeds of greatness—not the fruit but the seed. Whenever God gives anything He communicates it in seed form— whether it's a talent, an idea, or even His Word. *"Here is another illustration Jesus used: 'The Kingdom of Heaven is like a mustard seed planted in a field. It is the smallest of all seeds, but it becomes the largest of garden plants; it grows into a tree, and birds come and make nests in its branches.'"* [4] **All great things begin in seed form.**

But understand this: even though God supplies the seed we're all responsible for producing the fruit. Ultimately we're all accountable for how we handle His investment! *"It's also like a man going off on an extended trip. He called his servants together and delegated responsibilities. To one he gave five thousand dollars, to another two thousand, to a third one thousand, depending on their abilities. Then he left. Right off, the first servant went to work and doubled his master's investment."* [5] Notice it was the **servant** who went to work and *"doubled his master's investment."* The story continues with the first two being profitable and the master promoting them. But the third servant simply hid his master's investment and gave it back to him—every cent of it! Needless to say the boss wasn't thrilled with that: *"The master was furious. 'That's a terrible way to live! It's criminal to live cautiously like that! If you knew I was after the best, why did you do less than the least?!'"* [6]

Again, there are seeds of greatness inside of you and they need to be cultivated! Paul spoke about it when he said, *"We have this treasure from God, but we are like clay jars that hold the treasure. This shows that the great power is from God, not from us."* [7] In other words, "There's something in me, that's so much greater than me, that I know it couldn't be from me." You were meant to be great!

Quantitative vs. Qualitative Greatness

Greatness is broken down into two categories: qualitative and quantitative. It's possible to be quantitatively great and not qualitatively great, and vice versa. The differences are as follows:

a. **Quantitatively Great**—the external appearance of greatness. In the eyes of many this would be money, prestige, power, and the like.
b. **Qualitatively Great**—the internal attributes of greatness. These would be the character traits of love, joy, peace, patience, kindness, goodness, faithfulness, gentleness, and self-control. [8]

It's possible for someone to have both, just one, or neither. In my opinion, its commendable if one aspires to possess both; however, if you had to choose between the two—be a person of quality. A person with more quality than quantity can still enrich the lives of many. A person with more quantity than quality is like a bounced check—they give the appearance of wealth but inside they're broke! In fact, God is more concerned about your inner person than He is your outer person: *"What matters is not your outer appearance— the styling of your hair, the jewelry you wear, the cut of your clothes—but your inner disposition. Cultivate inner beauty, the gentle, gracious kind that God delights in."* [9]

Stephen Covey breaks greatness down in a similar fashion: **primary greatness** and **secondary greatness**. Over the past few years the world has witnessed the devastation as honesty, integrity, and the like were substituted for quick gain, lying, and deceit. Covey in a recent interview, delved deeper into his definitions of greatness and the effect their neglect had on the world at large:

"Financial success—prestige, wealth, recognition, accomplishment—will always be secondary in greatness. Primary greatness is about character and contribution. Primary greatness asks, What are you doing to make a difference in the world? Do you live truly by your values? Do you have total integrity in all your relationships? And when correct principles are not followed or ignored, the results can be catastrophic as we have witnessed the past year in the financial markets." [10]

You Become Great for Others

The Bible says, *"David perceived that the Lord had established him king over Israel, and that He had exalted his kingdom for His people Israel's sake."* [11]You were meant to be great, but know this: that greatness is not for you—it's for those around you. When God truly raises up someone He does it for the sake of others. The Queen of Sheba understood this. She heard about the wisdom of King Solomon and went to see if the reports were true. When she herself heard his wisdom, saw the palace he built, his wealth, his servants, and the worship services she was breathless. *"She said to the king, 'It's all true! Your reputation for accomplishment and wisdom that reached all the way to my country is confirmed. I wouldn't have believed it if I hadn't seen it for myself; they didn't exaggerate! Such wisdom and elegance—far more than I could ever have imagined. Lucky the men and women who work for you, getting to be around you every day and hear your wise words firsthand! And blessed be God, your God, who took such a liking to you and made you king. Clearly, God's love for Israel is behind this, making you king to keep a just order and nurture a God-pleasing people.'"* [12]

The talents you have, the tests you've been through, and the resources you've been given were never meant just for you. Life was designed in such a way that whatever we give away we gain more of and whatever we hoard we lose. Solomon spoke about this when he said, *"There is one who scatters, yet increases more; and there is one who withholds more than is right, but it leads to poverty. The generous soul will be made rich, and he who waters will also be watered*

23

himself." [13] People of greatness understand that they're born for others—their greatness lies in helping others to become great. They "die" so that others can live. Jesus said, *"Listen carefully: Unless a grain of wheat is buried in the ground, dead to the world, it is never any more than a grain of wheat. But if it is buried, it sprouts and reproduces itself many times over. In the same way, anyone who holds on to life just as it is destroys that life. But if you let it go, reckless in your love, you'll have it forever, real and eternal."* [14]

If You Don't Understand the Lesson, You Won't Pass the Class

"Hear me brothers and sisters, He is not a respecter of persons, but He is a respecter of principles. It doesn't matter who you are, God is no respecter of persons but He is a respecter of principles. And if you don't learn the principles regardless of who you are as a person He will keep sending you back to the first grade until you master the principle."—T.D. Jakes *[15]*

Imagine a school in which God is the Teacher of every grade and every subject. In this school are students from all around the globe—all cultures, colors, races, sexes, languages, and the like. He doesn't give out variations of grades (no A's, B's, or the like) just a green P (Pass) or red F (Fail). Any student who doesn't pass His class doesn't go to the next level or grade. The next level represents greater knowledge of the subject and as a result greater responsibilities. Some students in His class are older than the rest because of being forced to repeat the class. Despite the calls from parents, the uproar of the community, and the anger from the students themselves He has refused to just "pass" them through. "Until they truly learn My lesson," He says, "they will never pass My class!"

Tim and Billy

The classrooms are similar to each other: giant blackboard in the front, teacher's desk on the right, 28 identical desks grouped in rows of 7, lockers in the back for students, a larger locker for the Teacher, a row of windows on the left, a clock above the lockers behind the students, and a big wooden sign above the blackboard with an inscription: **to know something is to do the thing one knows**. The Teacher would often point to the sign and say to the class, "If you learn this and apply it to My lesson you'll have learned My lesson."

Now in one particular classroom there are two boys who have repeated the grade a multitude of times: Timmy Teachable and Billy Satisfied. They both came into the class at the same time and because the two have spent considerable time together they've became good friends. They're also the silent laughter of the class (silent because they're much older than everyone else...and as a result much stronger). It breaks the Teacher's Heart to see them come back year after year especially since He knows the potential in each of them. But though His heart breaks with compassion His rule remains inflexible: pass and you'll be promoted—fail and I'll see you here next year.

At the beginning of this particular year Tim meets with Billy:

"Billy, I'm tired of this. I'm tired of failing this class," Tim says. "We know His lesson inside out and I can't understand why we're not passing."

"Yeah I know. Why doesn't He just pass us already…I'm tired of being here. He just likes to see us suffer. It's His fault why we're still here."

"Nah…that can't be it…you know He's not partial. Maybe…maybe…it's something wrong with us."

"Us?? Nah man! Something's wrong with Him. I even went to ask Him what's going on. All He kept saying was 'Billy you have so much potential…it breaks My Heart to see you here' blah, blah, blah. Then He said something… what'd He say again…He said ummmmm…Oh yeah… 'live what you learn and you'll learn what you've lived.'"

"What was that last one?" Tim asked with piqued curiosity. "'Live what you what??'"

"Why what happened??" Billy asks curiously, unable to see the truth before his eyes.

"Just say what He said again!"

"He said, 'live what you learn and you'll learn what you've lived.'"

"Billy, I think that's it!! Maybe…He doesn't want us to just know the lesson but to *know* it," Tim said. He's still unsure of what he's stumbled on but he knows it's something. "Like I said….maybe the problem's not with Him… maybe it's with us?"

"Tim, the only problem we have is a Teacher who doesn't want to pass us," Billy said flatly. "Nothing's wrong with us, we know what He's teaching, we can handle the added responsibilities…although I'm not sure if I want to…He just doesn't want to pass us."

"Listen why don't we try to work harder?" asks Tim with a gleam in his eye. "Let's ask those who've passed what they did, what He wants, and let's just do it!! It may, you know, be a bit harder but I think if we really focus on it, work on ourselves, try to practice what He's teaching…I think we can get it done. Come on man, I think we can do it."

"'Do extra work?' 'Work on ourselves?' I'm not sure if I'm with that. I mean I don't like this whole thing...but that just seems like too much. Nah, I'm not with it. I think I'm just gonna complain some more, maybe get my folks involved, you know maybe they can push His Hand a bit. Maybe I can just get the answers from one of the smart kids?"

"Please Bill we can do this man! We can do it together!"

"Listen Tim you do it your way and I'll do it mine."

And with that Tim is true to his word. He starts by asking those who've passed what they did. At first he expects no one to help—he was willing to deal with a couple of rejections, but is shocked to find that those he asked were more than willing to help! They saw his eagerness and sincerity and wanted to assist. They remembered what the Teacher told them when they passed. As Tim grew in knowledge his habits changed. Everyone in the class begins to notice the difference in Tim including Billy.

The Grade

It's now the end of the year, and the Teacher hands out the grades. His practice has always been to hand out the grade and ask the student to leave. He knew giving it in the class would tempt those who passed to look down on those who failed, and those who failed to envy those who passed. After some time the only two students left in the class are Tim and Billy. The Teacher stands up from His desk, walks over to them, and addresses them both:

"You know how I've labored with both of you to learn My lesson. I know both of you have potential, talents, dreams, and so forth but **no one** graduates from My class just because they have potential. Only by learning what I teach will anyone pass My class." With that He hands both of them a folded sheet of paper, turns around, walks to the door, and motions with His Hand, "Good day gentlemen."

The two boys glance at each other, get up, walk down the row of desks, walk past the Teacher, walk into the hall, and hear the door close behind them. It's the last day of school so the hallway is practically empty except for a few students walking towards the exit.

"I can't take the suspense anymore," says Billy. With that he opens his paper and finds a red "F" in the middle of it. He reads the comments from the Teacher—the kind he's received year after year: "'smart...potential...learn My lesson and you'll pass this class' blah, blah, blah. Oh well, the work's too hard in the next grade anyway, too much responsibility. Who needs it?! Open yours Tim!"

Tim looks at the paper and his heart flutters as he opens it. In the middle of it is a big green "P." He reads the Teacher's comments to himself—'great improvements...I knew you could do it...you've learned this lesson...don't forget to serve...be ready to share the truth with those who want to know....congratulations.'

Billy is shocked as he looks at the passing grade! He looks at Tim, looks at the paper, grabs it out of Tim's hand, reads the comments, and looks back at Tim. "What? You passed? No, that's a mistake! You cheated didn't you? Yeah, that's it you cheated!! That's not fair!!" By this time the hallway is deserted and all they hear is the echo of Billy's last comment.

"I didn't cheat, Billy." Tim started. "I simply learned what He was trying to teach us. I...we...could've learned this years ago, but we refused to be taught. I just didn't want to go back in that class again."

"No you cheated, that's the only way you passed. You think you're better than me now don't you? Don't you?!"

"I'm not better than anybody and I didn't cheat," Tim said a little more angrily. Realizing his tone and seeing the despair in his friend's face he brings it down a notch, "Look Billy, I'll be more than willing to show you what I did, so you can get out too. If I can do it so can you."

"Nah that's ok," says Billy as he hands back the sheet of paper. "I don't need to go to that next grade anyway. I'm used to it here. Besides I'll find new friends. I don't need to hang out with cheaters anyway." Billy breaks away from Tim and with a quicker pace walks toward the exit.

"Please Billy," Tim pleads. "I'll be more than happy to help you."

"Thanks but no thanks." Without even looking at Tim, Billy gives a wave with his hand. "Catchya later, cheater!"

Billy never did graduate from that class and never did understand what the Teacher wanted. He made new friends and together they found multitudes of people to blame for where they were. Tim, on the other hand, continued his ascent and went on to do greater things. What Billy failed to realized was that the Teacher wasn't looking for knowledge of the lesson plan, but obedience to it. Both Tim and Billy knew what the Teacher taught but only one was willing to apply what he learned. And so it remains: to pass His class is to learn His lessons through obedience.

GROUP DISCUSSION QUESTIONS

"How excellent are the Lord's faithful people! My greatest pleasure is to be with them." [16]

1. What is your definition of greatness?
2. Who can you help make better? Who can you serve?
3. What is stopping you from cultivating your seeds of greatness? Fear? Doubt? Indifference?

4. Are you focused on being quantitatively great or qualitatively? What is the proper perspective to have?

5. What lessons do you need to learn to pass the Teacher's class? What has stopped you thus far?

3

PRINCIPLES

"Blessed are the undefiled in the way, who walk in the Law of the Lord...Give me understanding, and I shall keep Your Law; Indeed, I shall observe it with my whole heart." [1]

"Man's ability to fulfill his purpose and to be all God intended him to be is predicated on the requirement that he obey the principles God established when He created human beings. Why is this true? God is a God of principles. Everything He created was established to operate by certain principles that guarantee its proper function. This pattern in creation includes human beings. We were created to operate by principles that God established before He created us."—Myles Munroe, *The Purpose and Power of Praise & Worship*

L ike the scenario of the classroom no one graduates until they learn the lesson. People are raised up as they learn and apply certain time-tested principles or natural laws. God is no respecter of persons but He is a respecter of principles, and those who choose to operate in those principles He promotes.

When Cain and Abel brought offerings to God, God accepted Abel's offering but rejected Cain's. And Cain was angry that God had rejected Him; God noticed it and spoke to Cain about his attitude: *"'Why are you so angry?' the Lord asked Cain. 'Why do you look so dejected? You will be accepted if you do what is right. But if you refuse to do what is right, then watch out!'"* [2] In other words, "I accepted Abel because He did the right thing. If you do the right thing I'll also accept you. If you don't I won't!" God is no respecter of persons. The Bible says, *"If anyone competes...he does not win the prize unless he competes according to the **rules**."* [3] Principles are the rules; they're the guidelines.

Principles are natural laws that govern the world. They're timely, timeless, inflexible and will always produce a certain outcome. These natural laws are self-evident, much like the **law of gravity** and the **law of cause and effect**. Regardless of whether you believe in them or not they're there! If you don't believe in the law of gravity jump off a building—I guarantee your faith will be restored! The wise person aligns his or her life around correct principles. Jesus said, *"Anyone who listens to My teaching and follows it is wise, like a person who builds a house on solid rock. Though the rain comes in torrents and the floodwaters rise and the winds beat against that house, it won't collapse because it is built on bedrock. But anyone who hears My teaching and doesn't obey it is foolish, like a person who builds a house on sand. When the rains and floods come and the winds beat against that house, it will collapse with a mighty crash."* [4]

Principles vs. Practices

Rather than seek and apply timeless principles the vast majority seek "the quick fix." Why? Principles benefit the most over the **long term** but many are into the short-term, give-it-to-me-now way of living that gratifies for the moment but never satisfies over the long term. Such living carries with it short-term pleasure but long term harm. Fortunately in the end, principles always win and unlike a passing fad they never go out of style.

Great things lose their greatness by forsaking time-tested principles for the next "in" thing. To forsake principles for practices is like nursing a tree from the ground, watching it grow to great heights, and then taking an axe and chopping away at the base. "Why would anyone do that?!" you might ask. "Why grow something to be so great and then try to destroy it?" As ridiculous as it sounds, that's what many do when they give up time-tested principles. They think it won't make a difference...but sooner or later their actions do catch up. They don't see the effect immediately but sooner or later the tree will fall, and it falls *"with a mighty crash!!"* Principles are not practices as practices do change, but principles must be practiced in that principles do not change.

Our Knowledge of Principles is Innate

Deeply embedded in us is the knowledge of these natural laws. Even though our understanding of them is limited we have a sense that they exist and that violation of them has consequences. Paul says, *"When outsiders who have never heard of God's Law follow it more or less by instinct, they confirm its truth by their obedience. They show that God's Law is not something alien, imposed on us from without, but woven into the very fabric of our creation. There is something deep within them that echoes God's yes and no, right and wrong."* [5]

He also spoke about the "sin principle" he struggled with. When he wanted to do good he always found himself doing evil instead: *"However, it is no longer I who do the deed, but the **sin [principle]** which is at home in me and has possession of me. For I know that nothing good dwells within me, that is, in my flesh. I can will what is right, but I cannot perform it. [I have the intention and urge to do what is right, but no power to carry it out.] For I fail to practice the good deeds I desire to do, but the evil deeds that I do not desire to do are what I am [ever] doing. Now if I do what I do not desire to do, it is no longer I doing it [it is not myself that acts], but the **sin [principle]** which dwells within me [fixed and operating in my soul]. So I find it to be a law (rule of action of my being) that when I want to do what is right and good, evil is ever present with me and I am subject to its insistent demands."* [6]

Why is it that children with no knowledge of the justice system will cry out when wronged "that's not fair?!" How is that we, in secret, will say to those closest to us, "you know I need to be better than this?" Why is it that in the middle of doing wrong we often say, "I better quit, this is gonna catch up to me?" It's because somewhere in our makeup is the knowledge that these principles are inviolable and that their rewards or consequences are certain.

Principles are Practical

Principles were meant to be practiced and obeyed. David said, *"The **signposts** of God are clear and point out the right road. The **life-maps** of God are right, showing the way to joy. The **directions** of God are plain and easy on the eyes."* [7] That's what principles are: they're signposts and life maps; they're the invisible structures that give the visible world shape. They point us in the right direction, the right way. Stephen Covey once said, "Principles are like a compass. A compass has a true north that is objective and external, that reflects laws or principles, as opposed to values that are subjective and internal. Because the compass represents the verities of life, we must develop our value system with deep respect for 'true north' principles." [8]

"Therefore the law was our disciplinarian until Christ came, so that we might be justified by faith." [9]

When Paul spoke about the Old Testament Law he was inadvertently speaking about natural laws. The word "disciplinarian" is the Greek word "paidagogos" (pronounced PAHEE-DAG-O-GOS) where we get "pedagogue." Pedagogue has two meanings:

1. A teacher of children or youth
2. One (as a slave) having charge of a boy chiefly on the way to and from school in classical antiquity.

So the purpose of the pedagogue was to control and supervise the child through constant discipline. He would direct the child in the proper way to go. And so it is with principles: they're meant to teach us, supervise us, and put us on the right path. But their ultimate purpose is to point back to their Creator.

Criteria for Identifying Principles

With the abundance of practices that pose as principles, how do you determine which is which? How do I tell what is a temporary fleeting practice and what is a time-tested principle? Outlined are three criteria to determine whether something is a practice or a principle:

a) Principles are **immutable**—"Immutable" means "unchanged and unchangeable as to character and nature." Principles don't change. They don't love us one minute and hate us the next. They're constant and consistent and because of their consistent nature we can rely on a consistent outcome. With them *"there is nothing deceitful...nothing two-faced, nothing fickle."* [10]

b) Principles are **consequential**—If principles are followed they will (over time) bring rewards that are consistent, and if disobeyed will bring consequences that are equally consistent. If we obey them their rewards will be our help if we disobey them their consequences will be our downfall. Oh behold the goodness and severity of principles—to those who obey goodness and to those who disobey severity. They *"render to every man according to his deeds."* [11]

c) Principles are **universal**—They work for anybody regardless of culture, color, etc. They don't belong to a certain religious group, they don't just work for one person they're applicable to all. The Bible says, *"When Joshua was near Jericho he looked up and saw a man standing in front of him with a drawn sword in his hand. Joshua went up to him and asked, 'Are you for us or for our enemies?' 'Neither,' he replied."* [12] That's how principles work—they are neither for us nor against us. But they **work with us** when we **work with them**.

GROUP DISCUSSION QUESTIONS

"You are better off to have a friend than to be all alone, because then you will get more enjoyment out of what you earn. If you fall, your friend can help you up. But if you fall without having a friend nearby, you are really in trouble. If you sleep alone, you won't have anyone to keep you warm on a cold

night. Someone might be able to beat up one of you,
but not both of you. As the saying goes, 'A rope made
from three strands of cord is hard to break.'" [13]

1. What are principles?
2. What are the benefits of applying principles in every
   area of your life?
3. What's the difference between a principle and a
   practice?
4. How do great things or people lose their greatness?
5. What are the criteria to determine a principle?

4

ISOLATION

*"For this is the will of God even your **sanctification**..."* [1]

"Never before have I written a letter this long (or should I say a book?), I'm afraid that it is much too long to take up your precious time. I can assure you that it would have been much shorter if I had been writing from a comfortable desk, but what else is there to do when you are alone for days in the dull monotony of a narrow jail cell other than write long letters, think strange thoughts, and pray long prayers?" —Martin Luther King Jr., *Letter From Birmingham City Jail*

Sanctification is "the process of making holy for sacred use." It also means "to set apart for special use." In a literal sense, believers go through a process of sanctification where they're consecrated for His service through the Word and His Spirit. In a figurative sense, items are consecrated and set apart for His service. But in another sense, as it relates to being raised up, it's the inability to fit in.

People who do great things tend not to fit in. No matter how hard they try they just can't seem to mesh with the crowd. They stand out in some form or another (often to their despair). This can be seen in Moses who becomes an outsider because of his dual identity. He is a Hebrew raised in an Egyptian house—too Hebrew to be Egyptian and too Egyptian to be Hebrew. This is seen in Joseph who's an outsider with his brothers. This is seen in David who's somewhat of an outcast in his father's home. When Samuel asked Jesse if he had any more sons, hear Jesse's response: *"Well, yes, there's the **runt**. But he's out tending the sheep."* [2] Or what about Gideon? When called by God to deliver Israel listen to his response: *"Me, my master? How and with what could I ever save Israel? Look at me. My clan's the weakest in Manasseh and I'm the **runt** of the litter."* [3]

Or what about Jephthah? He became a judge over Israel…but for most of his life was scorned by those around him. He was the son of Gilead but his mother was a prostitute. Gilead's wife had other sons and when his half brothers grew up they chased him away. *"They told him, 'You will not inherit anything from our father; you are the son of another woman.'"* [4] He went away and soon became a leader of rebels. When Israel sinned against God and was conquered by the Philistines and Ammonites they called the outcast to lead them: *"When this happened, the leaders of Gilead went to bring Jephthah back from the land of Tob. They told him, 'Come and lead us, so that we can fight the Ammonites.' But Jephthah answered, 'You hated me so much that you forced me to leave my father's house. Why come to me now that you're in trouble?!'"* [5] The one who was scorned, rejected, and isolated ultimately gave Israel a tremendous victory and became one of its leaders.

In the future we call these people great; but in the present we call them weird or odd. For if it's not their appearance that's odd…it's just something about them that makes them different. They don't think like the masses, talk like the masses, or have the same interests as the masses. They have trouble with career paths because their true callings are not found in the classifieds. They just don't fit in. They weren't meant to fit in. They're not supposed to fit in. Their ideas don't fit in; their ideas are often ahead of their time and as a result aren't generally accepted. We look back and call them geniuses but we look now and call them idiots! They're the great but also the isolated.

But God has crafted them uniquely and distinctly for His own purpose. In fact, it's in times of isolation that He often does His best work:

- It's when Hagar is **alone** that God reveals Himself and shows His plan for her son. [6]
- It's when Jacob is **alone** that he wrestles with God and is given a new name. [7]
- Moses finds a Burning Bush on the backside of the desert **alone.** [8]
- The prodigal son comes to himself in a far country **alone.** [9]
- Paul writes most of the New Testament in a prison **alone**.
- John **alone** on the island of Patmos *"was in the Spirit on the Lord's day"* and writes the book of Revelation. [10] **God cultivates those He isolates.**

Yes We Can

"I was never the likeliest candidate for this office. We didn't start with much money or many endorsements. Our campaign was not hatched in the halls of Washington; it began in the back- yards of Des Moines and the living rooms of

Concord and the front porches of Charleston."—
Barack Obama

On November 4ᵗʰ, 2008 after a long and arduous presidential campaign trail millions around the globe turned their attention to Grant Park in Chicago waiting to see the victor and hear his speech. It was a moment packed with enthusiasm (and emotion, as even I fought back tears). The tens of thousands present burst into applause as the then president-elect walked onto the podium with family: his wife and two daughters. Dozens of cameras, camcorders, and camera phones were held up to take pictures of the man who on that night commanded the attention of the world. The crowd hushed as he began his victory speech:

> **"If there is anyone out there who still doubts that America is a place where all things are possible, who still wonders if the dream of our Founders is alive in our times, who still questions the power of our democracy, tonight is your answer. It's the answer told by lines that stretched around schools and churches in numbers this nation has never seen; by people who waited three hours and four hours, many for the very first time in their lives, because they believed that this time must be different; that their voice could be that difference."** [11]

Only time will tell whether this man who is now America's 44ᵗʰ president is equipped to handle the challenges that, at the time of this writing, currently grip this nation; only time will show what this president who speaks a bipartisan message will accomplish. But for the moment, as faith dwindles in the eyes of many a message of hope resounds in the ears of this nation and the world: yes we can!

Barack Hussein Obama Jr. is the first African American to be elected president of the United States. In a short span of time his meteoric rise to fame has astounded many political observers. His message of hope, crossing partisan lines, and building a greater America has resonated with people near and far. But judging from his present influence one could hardly imagine that he who represents so many once considered himself an outsider.

Now because Obama's story is so well known my purpose is not to echo his biographical call, but rather to show how isolation played its part in shaping his influence; to show how his once being banned from many circles caused him to eventually be embraced by many around the globe.

He was born August 4th, 1961 in Honolulu, Hawaii to Barack Obama, Sr. (a Kenyan foreign exchange student) and Ann Dunham (a student at the University of Hawaii). Though the two married on February 1961 they would divorce in January 1964 after Obama Sr. left his young family to further his education at Harvard University. Obama Jr. saw his father once more before his tragic death in 1982.

In 1963 his mother returned to school. Money was tight; she relied on food stamps and her parents to help take care of her young son. She later remarried to Lolo Soetoro, an Indonesian oil company manager. After her graduation she and Barack moved out to Jakarta. He attended a Catholic school, was registered as a Muslim (his stepfather's religion), and was the only foreigner there. In Indonesia he was teased and tormented relentlessly due to his size (he was bigger and better fed than most), his color, and language barrier (he never fully grasped the language). In fact, one time when he kept following a group of boys (who didn't want him tagging along) they grabbed his feet and hands and threw him into a nearby swamp. Fortunately he could swim. They would fight him, often ganging up on him, because he was hard to beat alone. He never did fit in with his classmates and would sit in a back corner alone. [12]

He returned to Hawaii in 1971 to live with his maternal grandparents. He attended the Punahou Academy and didn't seem to fit in there either. According to Bob Neer, "The new school was a shock: socially, culturally, and racially. Many of the other fifth graders had been together since kindergarten; Obama's Indonesian sandals were dowdy and his clothes out of style; and he was one of just two black children in the class." [13]

In ninth grade a young "Barry" Obama was befriended by Keith Kakugawa; in Obama's memoir he gave him the pen name "Ray." Kakugawa resurfaced again in his old friend's life during his presidential campaign, asking for money— he was recently released from jail and was homeless. In an interview with ABC News he talked about Obama's feeling of abandonment and isolation: "Everybody said they always saw him smiling and happy. I didn't. I got to see the turmoil, I got to see how he really felt. Here's a kid who was growing up as an adolescent in a tough situation. He felt abandoned, he felt that his father abandoned him and his mother was always pursuing her career." He then went onto say, "He is such a people person now, it's really amazing because he was a very, very shy—I wouldn't say introverted—but he was just a very shy, cautious kid." [14]

When he made an unsuccessful bid for the U.S. Congress in attempt to unseat Rep. Bobby Rush the doubts of many voters concerning his "blackness" rose to the surface— thanks in part to Rush's campaign. Rush's campaign basically argued that "Obama's not one of us." In fact, Donne Trotter, the state senator who also had his eye on the Congress chair, not only questioned Obama's "blackness" but also his white "connections." In the Chicago Reader Ted Klein wrote, "'Barack is viewed in part to be the white man in blackface in our community,' says Donne Trotter, who detests Obama.

'You just have to look at his supporters. Who pushed him to get where he is so fast? It's these individuals in Hyde Park, who don't always have the best interests of the community in mind.'" [15]

But yet somehow, someway his mixed heritage which was initially perceived as a curse was a blessing in disguise. Somewhere in between the struggle of being both black and white he found a home with both races. His multiracial background served as the key allowing him to open doors previously closed to others. According to David Mendell, during his run for senate and his sudden burst of fame, Obama himself was stunned by the sudden change of heart:

> "A fund-raiser thrown by a young black professional at a trendy downtown bar was packed to capacity. It took Obama half an hour to push himself through the crowd to the back of the huge nightclub, where he was to speak. When the host introduced him to the crowd as 'the best and the brightest we have to offer the world,' even the ambitious, self-assured Obama raised an eyebrow at this obsequious treatment. He needed a burly escort to help him back through the crowd and into the waiting SUV. Finally hopping back into the vehicle, he seemed stunned himself at the outpouring of affection." [16]

The fact that he felt isolated from the masses would end up bringing the masses to him. Obama, in hindsight, could appreciate the struggles that helped shape him: "I was raised as an Indonesian child, and as a Hawaiian child, and as a black and white child. Part of what I benefit from is a multiplicity of cultures that all fed me." [17]

"The Stone the Builders Rejected has Become the Capstone." [18]

I tried to think of some great example to bring this point home, some analogy so insightful that you the reader would read it, put the book down, and in a moment of contemplation say, "That's deep." I searched through Scripture, combed through books and articles trying to find something so profound that the scholar would have to nod his head in agreement, yet so simple that the everyday person could also agree. And then it hit me…the analogy I was looking for, one that would leave a far-reaching, deep, and profound impression. Are you ready? I hope you are…here it is…Rudolph the Red Nose Reindeer.

Hold on now! Hold on! Don't put the book down. Just hear me out! The story and the song has become an essential part of Christmas folklore. If you forgot the lyrics don't worry, I have them here:

"Rudolph, the red-nosed reindeer
had a very shiny nose.
And if you ever saw him,
you would even say it glows.

All of the other reindeer
used to laugh and call him names.
They never let poor Rudolph
join in any reindeer games.

Then one foggy Christmas Eve
Santa came to say:
'Rudolph with your nose so bright,
won't you guide my sleigh tonight?'

> Then all the reindeer loved him
> as they shouted out with glee,
> 'Rudolph the red-nosed reindeer,
> you'll go down in history!'"

Now let's look at this: Rudolph had a gift, a gift that originally alienated him from his brethren, but in time of adversity his gift proved the most useful, and the outcast went on to lead the very people who rejected him. I told you it was deep! Paul said to the believers in Corinth, *"Take a good look, friends, at who you were when you got called into this life. I don't see many of 'the brightest and the best' among you, not many influential, not many from high-society families. Isn't it obvious that God deliberately chose men and women that the culture overlooks and exploits and abuses; chose these 'nobodies' to expose the hollow pretensions of the 'somebodies?'"* [19]

If this resonates with you because you don't fit in, it may mean you're not supposed to fit in. Initially, the rejection is hard to take because we all seek to be accepted—but you are salt and light. And like salt you're meant to change whatever you're sprinkled on, and like light you're meant to give illumination to those that need it. Salt and light were never meant to fit in! Jesus said, *"You are the salt of the earth. But what good is salt if it has lost its flavor? Can you make it salty again? It will be thrown out and trampled underfoot as worthless. You are the light of the world—like a city on a hilltop that cannot be hidden. **No one lights a lamp and then puts it under a basket. Instead, a lamp is placed on a stand**, where it gives light to everyone in the house."* [20]

> *"God wasn't attracted to you and didn't choose you*
> *because you were big and important—the fact is,*
> *there was almost nothing to you. He did it out of*
> *sheer love..."* [21]

GROUP DISCUSSION QUESTIONS

"Keep company with the wise and you will become wise. If you make friends with stupid people, you will be ruined." [22]

1. Have you ever felt like you never fit in somewhere?
2. Why does God often isolate His chosen ones?
3. In hindsight, can you see the good in being isolated from certain groups?
4. Why is it that "salt and light" were never meant to fit in?
5. Are you focused on serving the "somebodies" of the world or the "nobodies" of the world? Can you see why God often chooses the "nobodies" or the "over looked?"

5

DESIRE

"Then I heard the Voice of the Lord saying, 'Whom shall I send, and who will go for us?' And I said, 'Here am I; send me!!'" [1]

"Desire is the starting point of all achievement."
—Napoleon Hill, *The Laws of Success*

No change or lasting achievement is ever birthed into existence without desire. Who can truly stop the person who desires something so much they're willing to stake all they have to acquire it? Not a hope, not a wish, not an attitude of indifference but a burning unquenchable desire that leaves you unsettled and uncomforted by anything less than your coveted goal. *"Appetite is an incentive to work; hunger makes you work all the harder."* [2]

Throughout history we see great people overcome adversity, face seemingly impossible circumstances, achieve their coveted goal, and are elevated from mediocrity to prominence. We, on the sidelines, watch these combatants and cheer enthusiastically when they finally win. We put them on pedestals and say things like: "They were more gifted, more talented, more knowledgeable, more experienced, they knew more people, had better advantages, and etc." However that is often not the case. Truth of the matter is, what separates these combatants is they wanted it more, believed they could have it, and didn't give up until they did.

People of Desire

Desire is essential as no great work will be accomplished **without** it. Ruth had **desire**. When Naomi told Orpah and Ruth to leave, Orpah left *"but Ruth replied, 'Don't urge me to leave you or to turn back from you. Where you go I will go, and where you stay I will stay. Your people will be my people and your God my God. Where you die I will die, and there I will be buried. May the Lord deal with me, be it ever so severely, if anything but death separates you and me. When Naomi realized that Ruth was determined to go with her, she stopped urging her."* [3]

David had **desire**. When David came down to the battle between Israel and the Philistines, and saw Goliath, and heard his taunts something inside of him bubbled up: *"Then David spoke to the men who stood by him, saying, 'What shall be done for the man who kills this Philistine and takes away the reproach from Israel? For who is this uncircumcised Philistine, that he should defy the armies of the living God?'"* [4] His desire and faith in God won him an "impossible" victory.

Blind Bartimaeus had **desire**. When he heard that Jesus was passing by he shouted to Him for help—he wanted to see. The people nearby scolded him—he was making too much noise. But he had too much desire to shut up: *"But he shouted even more loudly, 'Son of David, have mercy on me!'"* [5] His desire stopped Jesus right in His tracks! *"Jesus stopped and said, 'Call him!' They called the blind man and told him, 'Cheer up! Get up! He's calling you.' The blind man threw off his coat, jumped up, and went to Jesus. Jesus* asked him, *'What do you want Me to do for you?' The blind man said, 'Teacher, I want to see again.'"* [6] His desire and faith in God gave him his eyesight. With desire he called out to the Master and the Master in turn called right back.

A Canaanite woman had **desire**. Her daughter was afflicted by an evil spirit. At first Jesus ignored her, but the disciples begged Him to do something—she wouldn't quit and it was driving them crazy. When He met her He told her "no" but she refused to take "no" for an answer: *"Jesus said, 'I was sent only to the people of Israel! They are like a flock of lost sheep.' The woman came closer. Then she knelt down and begged, 'Please help me, Lord!' Jesus replied, 'It isn't right to take food away from children and feed it to dogs.' 'Lord, that's true,' the woman said, 'but even dogs get the crumbs that fall from their owner's table!'"* [7] Talk about a woman who wanted what she came after!

The Longer the Delay, the Greater the Desire

One of the ways God increases desire in your life is **to delay what you desire**. Paul told the church at Rome, *"And God, whom I so love to worship and serve by spreading the good news of His Son—the Message—knows that every time I think of you in my prayers, which is practically all the time, I ask Him to clear the way for me to come and see you. **The longer this waiting goes on, the deeper the ache**. I so want to be there to deliver God's gift in person and watch you grow stronger right before my eyes!"* [8]

God will often keep you away from the thing you desire to make you want it more! He knows how to turn up the heat! When He feels the temperature is right *then* He steps in—He wants to make sure **you want it** as bad as **He wants it for you!** *"A satisfied soul loathes the honeycomb, but to a **hungry soul** every bitter thing is sweet."* [9]

Desire Births Leadership

When Nehemiah heard the walls of Jerusalem were broken down—he knew he had to **do something**. And it was this desire to do something that drove him back to Israel; and he spearheaded the rebuilding of the wall. When Paul was in Athens *"his spirit was provoked within him when he saw that the city was given over to idols."* [10] He knew he had to do something. He went in that city and preached the Gospel—he got a mixed reaction: *"And when they heard of the resurrection of the dead, some mocked, while others said, 'We will hear you again on this matter.' So Paul departed from among them. However, some men joined him and believed, among them Dionysius the Areopagite, a woman named Damaris, and others with them."* [11] His desire to do something gained new believers and followers.

When a person sees an obvious need and has the desire to do something—them doing something births leadership. And it's not that the problems are invisible, it's just that they're the only ones willing to do something about it.

Another point: it's not wrong to desire a higher position, office, or level of influence; Paul says, *"...if a man desires the position of a bishop, he **desires** a good work."* [12] He then went on to speak about the qualifications necessary for such a position. There's nothing wrong in desiring a higher position, as long as it is achieved in the right way and maintained with the right character.

It's not a sin to desire greatness.

When the disciples argued among themselves who was the greatest Jesus never rebuked them. He only gave them instructions on *how* to be the greatest. And if you desire greatness as much as your lungs desire air you're sure to have it; its only he who hungers and thirsts that shall be filled. [13]

GROUP DISCUSSION QUESTIONS

*"So cheer each other up with the hope you have. Build each other up. In fact, that's what you are doing. Brothers and sisters, we ask you to have respect for the godly leaders who work hard among you. They have authority over you. They correct you. Have a lot of respect for them. Love them because of what they do. Live in peace with each other. Brothers and sisters, we are asking you to warn those who don't want to work. Cheer up those who are shy. Help those who are weak. **Put up with everyone.**"* [14]

1. Why do you think desire is the starting point of all achievement?
2. What do you desire to do? Who do you desire to help?
3. What needs do you see? What is the "something" you can do?
4. Is it wrong to desire a higher office or level of influence? Why? Why not?
5. Why did Jesus **not** rebuke His disciples for wanting to be great? What can we learn from that?

6

CHARACTER

"And not only this, but we also exult in our tribula-
tions, knowing that tribulation brings about perse-
*verance; and perseverance, **proven character**; and*
proven character, hope." [1]

"The character of the Christian worker is as
dear to God as the work he is doing, and no
pains must be spared by the Divine Craftsman
to complete the design to which He has set His
Hand."— F.B. Meyer, *The Life of Moses*

It is not enough to attain something without learning how
to maintain it. To attain something is the mark of stardom,
to maintain something is the mark of greatness. It takes a
Saul to attain a kingdom but only a David can maintain
it. God's purpose is to bring you to a state of permanence,
where you're *"steadfast, immovable, and always abounding*
in the work of the Lord." [2] Sound character is necessary for
maintenance and permanence.

Whatever you build will be built on the bedrock of your
character. If this bedrock is not under girded by sound principles and truth everything on it, in due time, will fall. Like

a house built on sand its demise is certain. Promotion is important but not nearly as important as the formation of sound character. Character is the primary focus, promotion is the secondary—not the other way around. Rick Warren understands this: "Much confusion in the Christian life comes from the simple truth that God is far more interested in building your character than He is anything else...God is far more interested in what you are than in what you do. We are human *beings*, not human *doings*. God is more concerned about your character than He is your career, because you will take your character into eternity not your career." [3]

God had to remind King Solomon about this very thing. While Solomon was engaged in building His Temple God wanted to make sure he understood the main focus: *"The word of God came to Solomon saying, 'About this Temple you are building—what's important is that* **you live the way I've set out for you and do what I tell you,** *following My instructions carefully and obediently. Then I'll complete in you the promise I made to David your father. I'll personally take up My residence among the Israelites—I won't desert My people Israel.'"* [4] God has always been more concerned about your character than your career.

From Process to Promise

Character growth is a slow *process* but is necessary for the *promise*. The process itself can take years but the promise can happen in a moment. When one does step onto the stage of notoriety, the world cries "They've arrived!!" But that arrival came only after a long steady journey filled with heartache and hardship. Promotion can happen in a moment but the process necessary for it can take so much longer.

Joseph endured the process of slavery and imprisonment for years *but in a moment* was elevated to the second in command behind Pharaoh. Job endured the loss of his wealth, the death of his children, the affliction of his body, the scorn of his neighbors, and the sharp tongue of his friends for an unknown period of time *but in a moment* had everything restored to him two-fold. David endured isolation, banishment, and the fear of death for years *but in a moment* was ushered to the throne on the shoulders of the people. Israel endured the unbearable cruelty of slavery for more than 400 years *but in a moment* of a few weeks went from a bound people to a freed nation. *"Weeping may **endure** for a night but joy **comes** in the morning."* [5]

Many shy away from the idea of sound character because of imperfections. But every person of sound character is not without faults. Sound character is not perfect character. One preacher said, *"Indeed, there is not a righteous man on earth who continually does good and who never sins."* [6] A perfect God uses imperfect people to perform His perfect will! (Try saying that five times fast!)

People with the soundest character have their balance sheet filled with assets **and** liabilities. Their gardens carry **both** wheat **and** tare. Don't let your flaws stop you! Simon (water) can't be severed from Peter (Rock); and the God of Israel (Prince) is also the God of Jacob (trickster).

David: Imperfect Man/Sound Character

Character in many instances has been reduced to the definition of integrity. That is accurate in part but not in whole, especially as it relates to attaining and maintaining promotion. A person can be morally sound but professionally incompetent. T.D. Jakes says it like this: "Good character is more than great morals. It is possible to be morally upstanding and still not exhibit the character that makes you an asset to an employer and a recipient of promotion." [7]

To take a better look at the concept let's use David as a case study. In David we find a man destined for greatness yet processed in the furnace of affliction, as all great people must be. In him we find strength and weakness, virtue and vice, saint and sinner. And yet we still find a man so committed to God that God calls him *"a man after His own Heart."* [8] So we'll break down character into four components:

- **Competence**
  "The hand of the diligent shall bear rule..." [9]

In order to do the tasks of your job you must have suitable skill, knowledge, experience, etc; they don't have to be exceptional but they must be adequate. Competence increases and is perfected through practice. Every teacher was once a student and every master a beginner. It was David's competence that allowed him to be promoted under Saul's leadership: *"And David went out and was successful wherever Saul sent him, so that Saul set him over the men of war. And this was good in the sight of all the people and also in the sight of Saul's servants."* [10] Competence is a necessity as people will not be ruled by someone who lacks it. Sheep demand a competent shepherd; men of war demand as leader a man of war. Jethro will demand that competent men be placed as judges to lighten the load of Moses. *"Do you see any truly competent workers? They will serve kings rather than working for ordinary people."* [11]

- **Capacity**
  "And no one puts new wine into old wineskins. For the old skins would burst from the pressure, spilling the wine and ruining the skins. New wine is stored in new wineskins so that both are preserved." [12]

The root meaning for the word "capacity" is "to hold much." [13] Capacity simply means that you can handle the present weight of responsibility with the possibility of an increase in weight and not *"burst from the pressure."* You can't have the glory of influence without the weight of responsibility. To have one is to live with the other—the two can't be severed. To escape the weight is to refuse the glory, and to seek the glory is to find the weight.

We're all born with the potential for great capacity, but only few realize this potential. These few are who we call leaders. They taste the fruits of influence because they're willing to accept the responsibility that comes with it. They make mistakes, but they make no excuses; they fail, but refuse to give up; they stumble, but refuse to fall; and if they do fall, refuse to stay down. Capacity never begins from outside it begins from within—never put the responsibility of increasing your capacity outside of yourself. Truly great people accept responsibility of their actions **and** the actions of those under them. As David leaps onto the pages of Scripture we see his capacity increase periodically—from his position as Saul's armor bearer to his ultimate role as king.

*   **Maturity**
    "But you are to be perfect, even as your Father in heaven is perfect." [14]

The word "perfect" is the Greek word "teleios" (pronounced TEEL-E-OSE) which also means "adulthood" or "maturity." So another way of saying this is "Be mature even as your Father in heaven is mature." Maturity is a necessity for leadership. When Paul describes the characteristics necessary for a bishop (or leader) he states point blank that the candidate must not be a novice

[15], but someone who is seasoned and more mature. In fact, the word "novice" is the Greek word "neophutos" (pronounced NEE-O-FOO-TOS) which is derived from two Greek words: "neos" (new) and "phutos" (planted). So a bishop (or leader) can't be someone who is newly planted but someone who is rooted and grounded; someone who can't be easily plucked up.

"Unlucky the land whose king is a young pup, and whose princes party all night. Lucky the land whose king is mature, where the princes behave themselves and don't drink themselves silly." [16] Even though David was anointed to be king of Israel at 17 he didn't take the throne of Israel until 37. He **had** to go through the process of maturation so that he could maintain what he attained. We live in a society of immediate gratification, where people want things yesterday. But God doesn't care how long it takes; He will delay His promises until He feels His chosen is mature enough to handle it! *"Here's a piece of bad business I've seen on this earth, an error that can be blamed on whoever is in charge: Immaturity is given a place of prominence, while maturity is made to take a backseat. I've seen unproven upstarts riding in style, while experienced veterans are put out to pasture."* [17]

Maturity doesn't just mean age, it also means mindset; the mindset of a child is vastly different from the mindset of an adult. Paul said, *"When I was a child, I talked like a child, I thought like a child, I reasoned like a child. When I became a man, I stopped those childish ways."* [18] To become an adult means to put away childish things. The child thinks of self while the adult thinks of others—no one who thinks exclusively of self can be an effective ruler in anything.

- **Integrity**

"...keep a sharp eye out for competent men—men who fear God, men of integrity, men who are incorruptible—and appoint them as leaders over groups organized by the thousand, by the hundred, by fifty, and by ten." [19]

Integrity means "steadfast adherence to a strict moral or ethical code" and "the quality or condition of being whole or undivided." What the latter means is that your moral beliefs are in line with moral action. What you say is what you do—your word is made flesh through consistent action. When David had two chances to kill Saul he didn't do it—he was a man of integrity. Even Saul recognized that David was a man of integrity. After David spared Saul's life listen to Saul's response: *"'Is that your voice, David my son?' And he wept aloud. 'You are more righteous than I,' he said. 'You have treated me well, but I have treated you badly. You have just now told me of the good you did to me; the Lord delivered me into your hands, but you did not kill me. When a man finds his enemy, does he let him get away unharmed? May the Lord reward you well for the way you treated me today. I know that you will surely be king and that the kingdom of Israel will be established in your hands.'"* [20] *"The Lord detests people with crooked hearts, but He delights in those with integrity."* [21]

If you question the validity of character look at the absurdity of its absence: who would promote a man with sub-par competence? How could he teach what he himself doesn't know? Why give a woman increased responsibility when she struggles under the weight of present responsibilities? Who would put the untested into prominence? Who, over the long haul, would trust somebody who lacks integrity? Sound character is a combination of all four: you have to be able to do your job, have the capacity for increased responsibility, be mature, and have integrity.

Do you lack in any of these areas? Good. Confession leads to correction. No one who formed sound character did it overnight. Only by learning lessons through mistakes, only through adversity and struggle meant for growth, only by obeying sound principles and truth, and only over a long period of time was their character forged. Can you have promotion without sound character? In my opinion: yes. Can you maintain it? In my opinion: no. Sound principles and truth will always lead to victory and permanence; the opposite leads to the opposite. Mohandas Gandhi once said, "When I despair, I remember that all through history the way of truth and love has always won. There have been tyrants and murderers and for a time they seem invincible, but in the end, they always fall — think of it, always." Character is necessary for the maintenance of promotion. For the believer, however, it is much more. Ultimately God uses time, truth, and trials to fashion character; but the character that is sought is the character of Christ.

GROUP DISCUSSION QUESTIONS

"So let's do it—full of belief, confident that we're presentable inside and out. Let's keep a firm grip on the promises that keep us going. He always keeps His Word. Let's see how inventive we can be in encouraging love and helping out, not avoiding worshiping together as some do but spurring each other on, especially as we see the big Day approaching." [22]

1. Why is God more concerned about who you are than what you do? Why does He care more about your character than your career?

2. Why is competence an important character trait? Why capacity? Why maturity? Why integrity?

3. If you lack a character trait why is it good to confess it? Be as honest as possible.

4. How does God form sound character in a person? How has He been forming it in you?

5. How important is character to maintaining something? Why?

7

LAW OF VISION

The law that states every plan, achievement, or purpose must be seen before it can be realized

"Where there is no vision, the people perish." [1]

"The way you *see* your life *shapes* your life."
—Rick Warren, *Purpose Driven Life*

The law of vision is as basic a principle as cause and effect. Those who obey it inevitably find themselves hoisted above any limitation (man-made or otherwise); while those who disobey it find themselves hopelessly trapped with no means of escape. The first rung up the ladder is **seeing** where you want to go. For the sake of clarity, the word "vision" will be defined as "the act or power of anticipating that which will or may come to be."

A man propelled in this life is a man with a vision for his life; a vision so strong that the picture on the inside surpasses the "reality" of the outside. When God commanded Moses to build the Tabernacle He told him to build it after the pattern he had **seen.** [2] And so it remains today, you can only build your life after the pattern you've seen for your life. When God spoke to Abraham about the land He'd give him, He told him all that he could **see** was his. *"After Abram and Lot had gone their separate ways, the Lord said to Abram: 'Look around to the north, south, east, and west. I will give you and your family all the land **you can see**. It will be theirs forever!'"* [3] Later when God wanted to show him how large his family would be He gave him a vision: *"Then He took him outside and said, 'Look at the sky. Count the stars. Can you do it? Count your descendants! You're going to have a big family, Abram!'"* [4] A vision is nothing but reality in seed form.

The Power of Goals

A vision is nothing but a daydream unless analyzed, written down, and made plain with the necessary steps for its realization. Once it is crystallized it must be realized through goals. The subject of goals has graced the pages of every inspirational book imaginable; thought leaders have disagreed on many things but are unanimous as it relates to goal setting and achievement; in fact the Bible says, *"Record the vision and inscribe it on tablets, that the one who reads it may run. For the vision is yet for the appointed time; It hastens toward the goal and it will not fail, though it tarries, wait for it; for it will certainly come, it will not delay."* [5]

Jack Canfield spoke about the power of goal setting: "Once you know your life purpose, determine your vision, and clarify what your true needs are, you have to convert them into specific, measurable goals and objectives and act on them with the certainty that you will achieve them. Experts on the science of success know the brain is a goal-seeking organism. Whatever goal you give to your subconscious mind, it will work day and night to achieve." [6]

One of the greatest gifts God ever gave human beings was a brain. People marvel at the power and intelligence of a computer but it was **the brain that built the computer!!** Despite rapid scientific progress much about how the brain works is a mystery. It's been estimated that humans only use 10 percent of the brain's power. That means 90 percent of immense potential lies untapped and underutilized. One of the ways to harness the latent potential of the brain is through goals.

The Reticular Activation System (RAS)

The brain receives millions of bits of information per second and that information goes through a filtering process—keeping some and deleting others. The Reticular Activation System is the brain's filter—it decides what to accept and what to reject based on values, beliefs, and prejudices. [7] The brain will only accept information that reinforces deeply held beliefs and reject those that don't. So whenever someone has a vision and that vision is made plain with goals, the RAS is activated to notice resources **and** filter in anything that will help achieve that goal. Often the resources were always there but never noticed. That's why psychologists have stated, "when a person is ready for a *thing it make its appearance.*" "It" only shows up when you're truly ready. When you're **not** ready you could be passing by "it" every day and never recognize it. There's also a proverb that says, "A man can walk in a forest and still not find timber wood!"

The brain is a "goal-seeking mechanism"— it will always guide you toward objectives. It derives its greatest pleasure from overcoming challenges. Caleb, one of the twelve scouts who spied out the Promised Land, and one of the two who believed they could have it, was an old man and he was still looking for challenges!! When Joshua was allocating the

Promised Land Caleb asked for a territory so he could drive out its enemies. He said, *"Today I am eighty-five years old. I am as strong now as I was when Moses sent me on that journey, and I can still travel and fight as well as I could then. So give me the hill country that the Lord promised me. You will remember that as scouts we found the descendants of Anak living there in great, walled towns. But if the Lord is with me, I will drive them out of the land, just as the Lord said."* [8] We're wired to complete objectives!

If that objective is to "get closer to God, lose weight, graduate college with a 3.5 GPA by June 2xxx, and etc" the brain will find ways and means to do that. The brain is engineered to accomplish. It's never satisfied until its moving toward some objective. But, be warned, the brain and RAS are neutral and will only filter in information that is in line with deeply held beliefs. If those values and beliefs are negative the brain will filter in information that reinforces those beliefs and reject any positive information that contradicts!

People of vision are always guided by that vision, and they focus their energies toward the attainment of their goal; they're not tossed to and fro with every idea or concept. They're willing to say "no" to things not in line with their vision and "yes" to things that are. *"**Keep your eyes straight ahead; ignore all sideshow distractions**. Watch your step, and the road will stretch out smooth before you. Look neither right nor left; leave evil in the dust."* [9]

The Importance of Clear Vision

To repeat, your vision must be made plain: where you're going, when you're going to get there, and what to do must be stated. The Bible says, *"If your goals are good, you will be respected."* [10] But keep in mind: goals are important but not as important as the goal setting. Goal setting allows you to clearly visualize what you want, to impress that image onto the brain, and to follow through on it. You may not accomplish the goal but it focuses the mind on "something!"

A vision to be effective must be clear, specific, measurable, and focused. There's a large difference between something **focused** and something **diffused**. Look at the example of sunlight and a magnifying glass. Sunlight is diffused and because it's diffused it brings heat. Now direct that same light through a magnifying glass and what happens? The light became a laser. That light now has the ability to cut through hard material. Something diffused brought **heat** while something focused brought **power**!

Your vision, in order to be effective, must be focused. Your vision **cannot** be a vague idea of what you *hope to have happen* but a detailed declaration of what you *expect to have happen*. It has to be yours. Only you know what you see. Your tabernacle can only be built with the detailed pattern or blueprint given to you.

Personal coach Laurie Beth Jones recalled an amusing experience she had with a client as it related to vision: "Last year I spoke on the phone with a client I have been coaching. A highly successful entrepreneur, he had a vague idea of what he wanted and needed to do in his life to take him to a higher level. He said he had read *The Path* but had not written down his answers to the questions. For his assignment I had him go back and write down the answers to the questions. In writing his vision specifically, he got very clear about what he wanted to create and experience in his life.

"I ran into him recently, and he was laughing exultantly. Everything he had written in his vision since our first discussion had come true—not in three years, but in ninety days. He said, 'As soon as I got clear about this vision thing—*wham!* Everything started coming to me so quickly. Now you need to write the next book to tell me what to do when all my vision starts coming true all at once.'" [11]

My "Vision Statement"

Some years ago, I worked with Avon as a representative (my first real stake in entrepreneurship). It was solely a commission-based job and it was my duty to grow my "business" by finding customers and selling my products. In the very early stages I remember attending a meeting held for reps in the NYC area. When I arrived I was impressed with the meeting place: it had a very appealing corporate décor. I've always been attracted to the business side of things and this only helped fuel the attraction.

The speaker (one of the company's execs) was a tall gentleman in a grey-pinstripe suit. His job was to revive us, refuel us, and push us to push our business. He talked about his rise from obscurity as an ordinary rep to his place of prominence. He sold the benefits and the abundance of opportunity available to the right person...or people who could grab it.

He wanted to help us to achieve our best. By this time I was fired up. I was sold. His enthusiasm was infectious and I showed signs of being contaminated. He then introduced us to an exercise: he wanted us to write down in plain language what we wanted to achieve in the business. He said to make it specific, detailed, and to make sure it meant something to us. I flipped open my pad and I wrote down my vision feverishly. I wrote: "I want to be a success in the business, get a lot of customers, and be all that God wants me to be." I was so impressed with my "detailed" vision that I immediately showed my supervisor. She took my pad, looked at my statement, glanced at me, gave me back the pad, and with a slight tone of indifference said, "That's nice."

Now over the years I thought about her response and two explanations came to mind. The first is that she didn't believe in my God and found it hard to marry the business to Him. The second, is that she being wiser knew what I wrote was not a detailed vision but a vague wish. And, in her wisdom, chose not to correct me because I wasn't at the stage where I could handle it. I'd like to believe it was the latter and not the former (even though I believe the former to be more reasonable).

What I wrote was not a vision statement; it was a warm fuzzy idea of what I wanted to have. It was not detailed, specific, or measurable. It wasn't plain so I couldn't run with it. Long story short, I failed in the business. The reasons for my failure were many: mismanagement of funds, no marketing strategy, working with bad clientele (the kind that liked to order but didn't like to pay), poor work ethic, and (the last and most important as it relates to this chapter) no idea of where I wanted to go.

Vision is Both Inside-out and Outside-in

Inside out— *"You're blessed when you get your inside world—your mind and heart—put right. Then you can see God in the outside world."* [12]

What you see outside is a reflection of what you are inside. For example: the positive see a positive world, the negative see a negative world, cheaters see a world of cheaters, and so on. People who cheat in a relationship tend to be the ones who accuse the other of cheating. Why? They simply project their own infidelity. You see what you are.

Never take too seriously the comments of others: "you're too fat," "you're too stupid," "you're too skinny," "you're too ugly," and etc. Often these comments are not accurate reflections but inaccurate projections. Comments like these are usually birthed out of the insecurities of the people making them. The insecure tear down while the secure build up.

The Bible says an interesting thing about marriage, it says husbands *"ought to love their wives as they love their own bodies. For a man who loves his wife actually shows love for himself. No one hates his own body but feeds and cares for it."* [13] If a person loves and respects their mate it shows that they love and respect themselves. And whatever is inside the person **that** is what the person will **see**. Many parents who never received love and affirmation in their youth tend to be overly critical of their own children. They find it hard to show love or any kind of support that would affirm their children's worth. Why? You can only give what you have.

Two people can be looking at the exact same thing and see something totally different. When Moses sent out twelve spies to view the Promised Land they saw the same thing but had a mixed interpretation. Caleb and Joshua believed they could have it but the other ten thought they couldn't. The majority gave a horrible report based on how they viewed themselves: *"The land through which we have gone as spies is a land that devours its inhabitants, and all the people whom we saw in it are men of great stature. There we saw the giants; and we were like grasshoppers in **our own sight**, and so we were in their sight."* [14]

Outside in—*"But friends, that's exactly who we are: children of God. And that's only the beginning. Who knows how we'll end up! What we know is that when Christ is openly revealed, **we'll see Him—and in seeing Him, become like Him.**"* [15]

Moses spent a lot of time in the Presence of God. It was there he vented his frustrations, acknowledged his weaknesses, and received orders on what to do next. When he came down from Mount Sinai he was unaware that his face was radiant. So because of his face, he covered it with a veil in the presence of the people but uncovered it in the

Presence of God. [16] Moses **saw** the radiance of God and **became** radiant himself.

We tend to become like whatever we view or study for a length of time. To see better is to become better, to see more is to become more, and to see greater is to become greater. The best way to ready people for their Promised Land is to give them glimpses of it. Jesus said, *"The eye is the lamp of the body; so then if your eye is clear, your whole body will be full of light."* [17] As it relates to vision there are two things that need to be addressed: the lens and the object. The lens refers to *how* we see and the object is *what we see.*

The lens is in direct proportion to the heart; when the heart is changed then the lens will change. The lens and object have to be in agreement in order to get the best picture. If the lens is dirty the picture will be flawed. But as we look at light through a clean lens our bodies can then *"be full of light."* So what does God do when He wants to change us? He first changes us from the inside out—changing our spirits, hearts, and minds so that we can see Him better. And then changes us from the outside in—tells us to focus on Him, His Word, and His promises so that we can become more like Him. To see better is to become better!

Why is it That…?

Why is it that a company or organization with a deeply entrenched long-term vision, seem to blow past competitors whose only ambition is to remain open? Why is it that the salesperson who can "close the deal" in his mind's eye will always surpass their counterparts who "hope" the prospect can see their products' value? Why is that the leader who envisions what **can be** seems to go further and gain more influence than those who only see what **it is**? Why is it that society seems to make a way for those who "know where they're going," while simultaneously pushing out of the way those whose actions prove otherwise? Why is it that resources, influence, and opportunity seem to tackle the man or woman of vision, while simultaneously dodging those who aren't sure what they want? It's because the law of vision is at work constantly producing rewards for obedience and consequences for disobedience. The proof of this law is littered throughout history in the lives of men and women who saw before they attained.

GROUP DISCUSSION QUESTIONS

"You are God's chosen people. You are holy and dearly loved. So put on tender mercy and kindness as if they were your clothes. Don't be proud. Be gentle and patient. Put up with each other. Forgive the things you are holding against one another. Forgive, just as the Lord forgave you. And over all of those good things put on love. Love holds them all together perfectly as if they were one." [18]

1. What does having a vision mean to you?
2. Why are goals important? How does the brain react to goal setting?
3. How important is a vision to an organization? A ministry? A company?
4. What is the vision for your organization? Ministry? Company?
5. What do you **see** for your life? Be honest. Be specific.
6. Why is a focused vision more effective than a diffused vision?
7. Why is it that those who have a vision seem to go farther than those who don't?

8

LAW OF THE EXTRA MILE

**The law that states one must be willing
to render more and better service than
immediately paid for with a pleasing attitude**

*"And whoever compels you to go one mile, go with
him two."* [1]

"Men suffer all their life long, under the foolish
superstition that they can be cheated. But it is
as impossible for a man to be cheated by anyone
but himself, as for a thing to be and not to be at
the same time. There is a third silent party to
all our bargains. The nature and soul of things
takes on itself the guaranty of the fulfillment
of every contract, so that honest service cannot
come to loss. If you serve an ungrateful master,
serve him the more. Put God in your debt. Every
stroke shall be repaid. The longer the payment
is withheld, the better for you; for compound
interest on compound interest is the rate and

usage of this exchequer."—*Ralph Waldo Emerson, Compensation*

The term "extra mile" has become a catch phrase to many; but it's significant in moving from the background to the forefront. When Jesus spoke about this principle He related its significance to an oppressive practice in His day. The practice originated with the Persian government under the rule of King Cyrus. Under this custom the king's messengers had power to take horses, camels, and men into service against their will. In fact, couriers or messengers were often staged in specific locations by the king; if a man were to pass this post an official could rush out and "compel" him into service. [2] This custom was then adopted by the Roman government. Simone of Cyrene was "compelled" into helping Jesus with His cross, when the weight became too heavy. [3]

Rather than quarrel and complain about this oppressive treatment, Jesus advises us to do otherwise. He not only advises us to comply with the request but to exceed expectations in a spirit of love and service. *"You have heard the law that says, 'Love your neighbor' and hate your enemy. But I say, love your enemies! Pray for those who persecute you! In that way, you will be acting as true children of your Father in heaven. For He gives His sunlight to both the evil and the good, and He sends rain on the just and the unjust alike. If you love only those who love you, what reward is there for that? Even corrupt tax collectors do that much. If you are kind only to your friends, how are you different from anyone else? Even pagans do that."* [4]

Attitude Determines Altitude

As you employ this law understand that **what you do** is as important as the spirit (or attitude) in **which you do it**. Paul said, *"Servants, respectfully obey your earthly masters* *but always with an eye to obeying the real Master, Christ. Don't just do what you have to do to get by, but work heartily, as Christ's servants doing what God wants you to do.* **And work with a smile on your face,** *always keeping in mind that no matter who happens to be giving the orders, you're really serving God. Good work will get you good pay from the Master, regardless of whether you are slave or free."* [5]

Go the extra mile with a cheerful attitude. Not a depressed, indifferent, or mad disposition because you feel like "you have to do it"—God doesn't honor that. *"The point is this whoever sows sparingly will also reap sparingly, and whoever sows bountifully will also reap bountifully. Each one must give as he has decided in his heart,* **not reluctantly or under compulsion, for God loves a cheerful giver.** *And God is able to make all grace abound to you, so that having all sufficiency in all things at all times, you may abound in every good work."* [6] The spotlight of attention shines favorably on those who put to use this principle. You soon become indispensable to superiors, because in contrast, others don't even go the first mile; and if they go, they do it with such a negative attitude it were better if they'd not gone at all.

The compensation of doing more than paid for is inevitable but not immediately apparent. Seed sown one day doesn't bring fruit the next. There's a waiting time. When harvest does come it never returns with just that seed but fruit that bears more seed: a two, three, five, hundred-fold investment. If the return is delayed how much better for you? For when the return does come it comes back with such **compounded interest,** that the waiting time pales in comparison!!

Paul also said, *"Servants, obey in all things your masters according to the flesh; not with eyeservice, as menpleasers; but in singleness of heart, fearing God; And whatsoever ye do, do it heartily, as to the Lord, and not unto men"* [7] The Greek word for "eyeservice" means, "service performed under the master's eyes." The word for "menpleasers" means, "studying to please man or courting the favor of men." Going the extra mile means not just doing it when the boss is around or doing it to court favorable attention (in fact…you'll court more unfavorable attention in the beginning). It means to do the best all the time whether somebody's looking or not.

We All Worked For Free

Most people don't like to go the extra mile because the rewards aren't immediate—they don't show up in next week's check! "Why would I do extra work and not be paid for it? I don't work for free!" That argument used to make so much sense to me until I realized that we all, at one point, worked for free!

Robert Kiyosaki tells of a time when his "rich" dad spoke to him about working for free: "…look at great athletes who earn a lot of money. I do not know of a single great athlete who got paid for practicing his or her sport. Most professional athletes started young, practiced longer and harder than the average athlete. Most professional athletes practiced for years, many paid for lessons, and they put in long hours, long before they got paid. They had to do their homework before they got their jobs as pros." He then went on to say, "Even the Beatles worked for free before they became world famous and rich. Like the medical doctor or professional, they paid their dues. They did their homework. They did not ask for a guaranteed recording contract, a steady paycheck, and medical benefits before they began practicing." [8]

People who go the extra mile are rewarded in due time. Exceed expectations whether you are immediately paid or not. The rewards for people who go the extra mile are greater than those who are only "paid" to go the first mile.

Look at Ruth. She went the extra mile for Naomi and left all she knew and followed her to Bethlehem. Was she paid the next day? No. But she was paid, in more ways she could've imagined! When she went to work in Boaz's field, to gather grain behind the harvesters, Boaz greeted her warmly, told her she was under his protection, and that she was free to drink the water from his wells. *"Ruth fell at his feet and thanked him warmly. 'What have I done to deserve such kindness?' she asked. 'I am only a foreigner.' 'Yes, I know,' Boaz replied. 'But I also know about everything you have done for your mother-in-law since the death of your husband. I have heard how you left your father and mother and your own land to live here among complete strangers. May the Lord, the God of Israel, under Whose Wings you have come to take refuge, reward you fully for what you have done."* [9]

After a break she went back to work and *"Boaz ordered his servants: 'Let her glean where there's still plenty of grain on the ground—make it easy for her. Better yet, pull some of the good stuff out and leave it for her to glean. Give her special treatment.' Ruth gleaned in the field until evening. When she threshed out what she had gathered, she ended up with nearly a full sack of barley!"* [10]

God blesses people who go the extra mile.

The Extra Mile Worked at Def Jam

Kevin Liles knows what it means to go the extra mile. The former president of Def Jam Records rose from unpaid intern to president in nine years. Liles adopted the principle of the extra mile and practiced it in every position he filled.

Beginning his career at Def Jam he reported to his supervisor Kevin Mitchell. Mitchell was new to the Baltimore area where Liles was born and bred. Liles had what Mitchell needed: knowledge of the area and connections in the area. Rather than use them to his advantage and outshine the boss, he used his resources to make the boss shine. For example Mitchell needed to meet with Baltimore's Frank Ski (the most popular DJ at the time). He was unknown and was refused access. Liles, however, made a way for his new boss: "I already knew Frank. We went way back to the days when he was deejaying in the clubs...So when Kevin asked for my help, it was simple. I went over to the station and called up to the studio. I said, 'Frank, I've got a new guy here from Def Jam, why don't you let him come up?' Frank said, 'Cool, no problem.'"

Liles continued to put the extra mile principle into effect, doing more than immediately paid for:

> "For two more years, I hustled hard. I wrote weekly play reports that were pure poetry...Everyday I got into the habit of entering everything into a computer so I would always know what had been done, and what needed to be followed up on. I focused all my efforts on Kevin Mitchell's behalf. Anything he needed, I got done, even if I had to spend my own money to be effective. If we needed to fill a venue with 2,000 people, I'd herd them in. If a radio program director needed to hear our latest release, I'd get it to him personally, with Kevin Mitchell's best wishes...I didn't have to brag. I didn't need to undermine Kevin Mitchell...To get noticed, all I had to do was play my position and serve my boss to the best of my ability. If you do that, you'll shine no matter where you're at in the food chain." [11]

Mitchell was soon promoted out of the Baltimore area and Liles was hired to a full time position with the company. He continued to use the extra mile principle and years later was promoted up the "food chain." Under his leadership Def

Jam's revenues leaped from $100 million to more than $400 million in the span of a few years. [12]

Mordechai Went the Extra Mile

Mordecai went the extra mile in saving King Xerxes from assassination. Look at what he did:

> *"One day as Mordecai was on duty at the king's gate, two of the king's eunuchs, Bigthana and Teresh—who were guards at the door of the king's private quarters became angry at King Xerxes and plotted to assassinate him. But Mordecai heard about the plot and gave the information to Queen Esther. She then told the king about it and gave Mordecai credit for the report. When an investigation was made and Mordecai's story was found to be true, the two men were impaled on a sharpened pole. This was all recorded in The Book of the History of King Xerxes' Reign."* [13]

No "thank you" was given. The king didn't even acknowledge him. Where's his reward? Even though Esther made sure to give Mordechai the credit, nothing happened. Ahhh... but something did happen: everything was recorded. Though extra mile actions aren't immediately rewarded they are immediately recorded. And the beautiful thing is no deed ever goes unnoticed, unresolved, or unrewarded. But let's get back to the story:

> *"That night the king had trouble sleeping, so he ordered an attendant to bring the historical records of his kingdom so they could be read to him. In those records he discovered an account of how Mordecai had exposed the plot of Bigthana and*

Teresh, two of the eunuchs who guarded the door
to the king's private quarters. They had plotted to
assassinate the king.

'What reward or recognition did we ever give
Mordecai for this?' the king asked.
His attendants replied, 'Nothing has been done.'" [14]

It's only a fool who believes that deeds, no matter how hidden, will continually be unchecked. "No one notices," they say. "And I'll get away with it." But *"He Who planted the ear, shall He not hear? He Who formed the eye, shall He not see?"* [15] Isn't there an invisible Judge that bears witness to everything? Isn't He the One Who, after seeing everything, puts down one and exalts another?

You are always being watched; whether it's the silent eye of your supervisor, coworkers, and peers know that no deed goes unnoticed. And if the deeds do escape them they never escape God's invisible Eye: *"Mark well that God doesn't miss a move you make; He's aware of every step you take."* [16] The reward may be delayed, but however long the delay, when the time for repayment does come it's as if God Himself sits up and asks: "What reward did we ever give him or her for that?!" And He refuses to rest until the question is answered and the reward, with its compound interest, is given. Back to the story:

"'Who is that in the outer court?' the king inquired.
As it happened, Haman had just arrived in the
outer court of the palace to ask the king to impale
Mordecai on the pole he had prepared.

So the attendants replied to the king, 'Haman is out
in the court.'

'Bring him in,' the king ordered. So Haman came in, and the king said, 'What should I do to honor a man who truly pleases me?'

Haman thought to himself, 'Whom would the king wish to honor more than me?' So he replied, 'If the king wishes to honor someone, he should bring out one of the king's own royal robes, as well as a horse that the king himself has ridden—one with a royal emblem on its head. Let the robes and the horse be handed over to one of the king's most noble officials. And let him see that the man whom the king wishes to honor is dressed in the king's robes and led through the city square on the king's horse. Have the official shout as they go, 'This is what the king does for someone he wishes to honor!'

'Excellent!' the king said to Haman. 'Quick! Take the robes and my horse, and do just as you have said for Mordecai the Jew, who sits at the gate of the palace. Leave out nothing you have suggested!'" [17]

Mordecai went the extra mile and it not only rewarded him, it saved his life, and helped in saving the lives of his people. And what's so great about this is that the reward came through Haman—the guy who wanted him dead!! Go the extra mile in everything you do!!

Vince Papale: A Man Who Became "Invincible"

One Saturday night my wife and I decided to stay home to watch a movie—my wife calls this "family time" and she is the biggest supporter. So we watched two movies that night. The first movie was really boring—we got through half of it and were like "next!" The second one, on the other hand, was unbelievable. We were glued to our seats, all incoming calls went to voicemail, and if one of us had to use the bathroom the other one would be a nag: "are you done yet?!" It was just that good. At the end of the movie, still spellbound by what I saw, I looked at my wife and, in reference to the main character, said, "That guy's going in the book!"

Walt Disney's *Invincible* was based on the life of Vince Papale a 30-year-old bouncer who defied all odds by becoming the oldest rookie for the NFL. He played for the Philadelphia Eagles from 1976-1978 before retiring due to injuries. In the movie, the Eagles hired a new coach, Dick Vermeil, to help revive the losing team—the franchise hadn't been to the playoffs in sixteen years and the city was desperate for a change. Vermeil decided to hold open tryouts in 1976 for a spot on the team's roster.

Papale, in the movie, was a part-time bartender and teacher but lost his teaching job. Then to make matters worse his wife left him, took all the furniture, and left behind a scathing note: **"Vince, you'll never go anywhere. You'll never make any money; and you'll never make a name for yourself."** At this low point his friends persuaded him to go to the open tryouts. At the tryouts, he caught the attention of Vermeil who invited him to training camp. Through incredible hard work, sacrifice, and going the extra mile he made the team.

Though Papale's story is exemplary, what stood out to me was his use of the extra mile principle and the negative backlash he received. In the movie, after the first training camp two of his potential teammates confront Papale in the locker room and the dialogue goes like this:

"What do you think you're doing out there, pops?" says the first teammate

"What?" says Papale

"It's the first day of camp, [you] might wanna settle down," says the second teammate. "Try helping out the ones who are actually gonna make this team."

The two walk away laughing and Papale looks around to see the angry faces of his teammates. In an interview Papale was asked was the resentment real—his answer: "Even more so. A lot of them were just indifferent, but some were hostile. I had to have my head on a swivel—I felt like the girl in The Exorcist. After all, they had this impeccable football pedigree, and here I was coming in with little or no football experience." [18] In another interview with *USA Today* he spoke about going the extra mile: "When you're a long shot, you have to do something every day to get noticed. Every time I caught the ball, I'd run 30 more yards downfield. That ticked off the defensive backs to no end. They thought I was showing them up. But that's what caught Vermeil's eye." [19]

When Papale went the extra mile the other teammates felt it made them look bad. Dennis Frank, Eagles center (1976-78), said this about Papale: "It was rather interesting to see him coming out there, a 30-year-old rookie, working so *hard* with this *huge* desire to make things happen but getting no respect."

After making the cut he soon made an impact on the team. Papale was instrumental in the Eagles first win over the NY Giants; and he was even made special teams captain. Some things in the movie were different from real life: in the movie he was a bartender—in real life he was a bouncer, in the movie he played no college football— in real life he started as receiver in the short-lived World Football League with the Philadelphia Bell giving him a lot of experience, in the movie his wife left him before he made the team—in real life she contends she was there, and etc. But what was absolutely true is that Papale employed the extra mile principle in everything and became an example to every one around him. ***"Hard work always pays off;*** *mere talk puts no bread on the table!"* [20]

> "He's a guy who had his shot. Who only wanted to go the distance—and became an inspiration; not only for the city but, I mean, Vermeil credits him widely with helping them restore a winning attitude back to the team"—Victor Constantino, Executive Producer, *Invincible*

Going the Extra Mile Can Bring Extra Problems

Understand this: most people don't go the extra mile—they go the first mile, then stop, and some don't even finish the first! They do enough work to stay under the radar. So when a person decides to do extra they feel threatened. When Kevin Liles went the extra mile at Def Jam he received criticism from coworkers, just like Vince Papale who received criticism from his team. When you go the extra mile expect to receive heat from those who only go one mile.

When I took a job at my uncle's restaurant as a delivery boy I made up my mind that I was going to be the best delivery boy he had. I did everything in my job description and more: if he needed me to get to a certain address in fifteen minutes I'd get there in ten. I cleaned and washed the car with my own money. I'd have the solution to a question before he asked it, I would clean around the restaurant in down times, and I did whatever I could to help him.

I soon caught the attention of my uncle and his staff. The staff unfortunately wasn't too happy about it. I'd get glares, snide remarks, and "advice"—"you don't need to be working that hard," "you're gonna hurt yourself doing all that," "where's the extra money—you're not getting paid for this," and so on. I listened to their "advice" and buckled under their criticism. I went back to going the first mile. I thought "yeah, where is the extra money?" "Why am I doing all this work?" I realized later how wrong I was. If I'd kept going the extra mile, who knows how far I would've gotten in my uncle's business? I doubt I would've remained the delivery boy! But I made the mistake of buckling under the pressure that doing extra brings. Don't make my mistake. Go the extra mile even if it brings glares, snide remarks, and "advice." Keep at it—don't quit.

GROUP DISCUSSION QUESTIONS

"In light of all this, here's what I want you to do. While I'm locked up here, a prisoner for the Master, I want you to get out there and walk— better yet, run— on the road God called you to travel. I don't want any of you sitting around on your hands. I don't want anyone strolling off, down some path that goes nowhere. And mark that you do this with humility and discipline—not in fits and starts, but steadily, pouring yourselves out for each other in acts of love, alert at noticing differences and quick at mending fences. You were all called to travel on the same road and in the same direction, so stay together, both outwardly and inwardly. You have one Master, one faith, one baptism, one God and Father of all, Who rules over all, works through all, and is present in all. Everything you are and think and do is permeated with Oneness." [21]

1. What are the benefits of going the extra mile?
2. What are some of the techniques Kevin Liles used in going the extra mile for his boss? What are some of the techniques you can use?
3. Are you currently going the extra mile? If not, why?

4. Are the benefits of the extra mile immediately apparent? Why is it good that there are delays in being rewarded?

5. The bosses for an organization are its customers, what are the benefits of going the extra mile for your bosses?

6. How was Mordechai rewarded?

7. What are some problems going the extra mile can bring? Why?

9

LAW OF PERSISTENCE

The law that states only through consistent and continuous effort can any plan, vision, or achievement be realized

"So let's not get tired of doing what is good. At just the right time we will reap a harvest of blessing if we don't give up." [1]

"Nothing in this world can take the place of persistence. Talent will not; nothing is more common than unsuccessful people with talent. Genius will not; unrewarded genius is almost a proverb. Education will not; the world is full of educated derelicts. Persistence and determination alone are omnipotent. The slogan 'press on' has solved and always will solve the problems of the human race."
—Calvin Coolidge, *30th President of the United States*

No outstanding achievement can be won without continuous effort. The wheel of fortune has a habit of turning slowly and it turns toward those who've proven through persistence that they deserve its rewards. Before you meet with any success know that you will meet with misfortune, mistakes, delays, and temporary defeats. Let this encourage you if you've tasted the fruit of adversity in all its wonderful flavors!

Why is it Always so Hard?

It all started when God cursed the ground because of Adam's disobedience. *"The Lord said to the man, 'You listened to your wife and ate fruit from that tree. And so, the ground will be under a curse because of what you did. As long as you live, **you will have to struggle to grow enough food.** Your food will be plants, but the ground will produce thorns and thistles. **You will have to sweat to earn a living.**"* [2] Before that it was easy to get what was needed, but disobedience shut that door. And now when we look for plants we get thorns and thistles first; because of this, no person achieves success without first being tested by adversity; and no adversity is overcome without persistence. Napoleon Hill had an interesting take on this subject:

> "There is no substitute for persistence. It cannot be supplanted by any other quality! Remember this and it will hearten you, in the beginning when the going may seem difficult and slow. Those who have cultivated the habit of persistence seem to enjoy insurance against failure. No matter how many times they are defeated, they finally arrive up toward the ladder."

He then went on to say: "Sometimes it appears that there is a hidden Guide whose duty is to test men through all sort of discouraging experiences. Those who pick themselves up after defeat and keep on trying, arrive; and the world cries, 'Bravo! I knew you could do it!' The hidden Guide let's no one enjoy great achievement without passing the persistence test. Those who can't take it simply, do not make the grade. Those who can 'take it' are bountifully rewarded for their persistence. They receive, as their compensation, whatever goal they are pursuing." [3]

Hill should know from firsthand experience, having spent more than **twenty years** in research on the philosophy of personal achievement, and having personally experienced "all sort of discouraging experiences."

Tyler Perry will shout "preach" when he read this knowing firsthand what it is to persist in spite of adversity. The actor, screenwriter, director, playwright, film producer, and television producer overcame abuse, poverty, homelessness, sexual molestation, and two suicide attempts to build a billion dollar entertainment empire. With determination, persistence, faith in God, forgiveness, and a feisty grandmother that brought audiences to tears with laughter he conquered all odds.

"I Know I've Been Changed"

He was born Emmitt R. Perry Jr. in New Orleans, Louisiana. His childhood was marked by poverty and physical abuse. In the Perry home Monday through Thursday were uneventful, but on Friday his carpenter and construction worker father would go out, get drunk, and per Perry "all hell would break loose." Perry Jr. often watched helplessly as Perry Sr., in a drunken rage, would beat his mother. After the beatings Perry Jr. would try and comfort his mother, and the two would often fall asleep crying. [4]

The beatings continued until one day his mother began fighting back (kicking, scratching, and punching)—the verbal abuse continued but Perry Sr. never again raised his hand against her. Perry himself was also a victim of his father's drunken rage. In addition to the beatings, he was dealing with the effects of molestation. He was molested by a man and woman in his neighborhood between the ages of five and twelve. At age sixteen Perry Jr. changed his name to Tyler: "I just started telling people my name is Tyler. I didn't want to carry my father's name. I didn't want to be anything like him. I didn't want to be his Jr. I have no idea where I got the name from." [5] Few knew the extent of the physical and mental abuse he suffered: "I remember when I was 17, I did something that ticked him off—something minor. My father grabbed me, threw me to the floor, and stomped me." He then went on to say, "Those were really sad times. There were times when I felt I wasn't going to make it. It was nothing but the grace of God that helped me make it through." [6]

Two things happened that changed his life: 1) an Oprah episode and 2) a trip to Atlanta. On that show Oprah told her viewers it was cathartic to write things down, so he began to journal the abuse he was suffering. He used different character names to maintain his anonymity. Out of that journal came his first play [I Know I've Been Changed]—it was about a character, which confronts an abuser, forgives him, and moves on. [7]

On his first road trip to Atlanta Perry was astounded by what he saw. To him it was Canaan. "I thought I'd gotten to the Promised Land," he says. "I'd never seen black people doing so well. I'd always thought—because I tried to speak well and represent myself well, and that didn't go over too well with the fellas in the 'hood—that I was crazy. But when I got here and saw other people doing the same thing, I said, 'I'm home!'" [8] He was ambitious and wanted more than the poverty he grew up in. He left New Orleans for Atlanta with the dreams of becoming a successful playwright.

With $12,000 in savings he rented a theater and produced his play—hoping to pocket $20,000. Only thirty people showed up the entire weekend. By the end of it he was broke, discouraged, and very angry. The Guide would not be avoided. [9]

Faith, Forgiveness, and Success

For the next six years Perry worked with different investors to finance his play (each production failed every time). [10] He networked with various ministries, produced the play through church appearances, he wrote, and rewrote. At times he was homeless, penniless, and jobless—he would often sleep in his Geo metro or small run down hotels. Friends and family members, fearful for his safety, would beg him to give up the theater and find a steady 9-to-5; but he persevered. Even though his play talked about forgiving one's abuser Perry had yet to apply its message. He still had resentment against the man who was his abuser—his father.

In 1998, Perry decided to have one more run of the play. He scheduled to present it at the House of Blues. Before the show he called his father and during their conversation Perry finally forgave his father. After that the show sold out! "Maybe I visited the right churches. Maybe I finally got the word out," he says. "But until I die, I'll believe that when I finally forgave my father, the Lord blessed the play." [11] Since then Perry has gone on from plays, to a syndicated TV show (House of Payne), and movies. In October 2008 he purchased a 200,000-square foot, 30-acre studio that was once the headquarters of Delta Airlines in Georgia. [12]

The Guide tested him and he passed the test. From then on the same Hand that held him back was the one that pressed him forward. And now the world cries, "Bravo! We knew you could do it!" Perry has since worked out his relationship with his father and the two have become good friends: "How can I be angry with this man when everything he did formed the man I am *and* I love the man I am today." [13]

> "I tell people, if you're thinking about suicide, all that stuff I've attempted and thought about it. If you think about it, life gets better. The key to life when it gets tough is to keep moving. Just keep moving."—Tyler Perry

Try a Different Strategy, But Don't Give Up

Most great ideas are variations of good ideas. Someone has a good idea, tries it, it doesn't work, makes an adjustment, tries it, it doesn't work, makes another adjustment, tries it, and it becomes a resounding success. It was the same idea just tweaked and improved. <u>One change of a variable can modify the whole equation.</u> That's why mistakes aren't bad; failure is crucial to success. Mistakes teach us what doesn't work so that we can make adjustments. Mistakes aren't bad **not learning** from mistakes **is** bad. But the benefits of mistakes and failures will only be realized with persistence. Tom Watson Sr., past president of IBM, once said, "If you want to increase your success rate, double your failure rate."

Jesus taught His disciples the value of trying different strategies. The first time, is when He called them to be His disciples. He was on the shore of Lake Gennesaret teaching a crowd. He saw two boats and got into the one that was Simon Peter's—Simon was washing the fish nets, an indication that He was done for the day. Jesus got into the boat that belonged to Simon and asked him to row it out a little way from the shore.

"Then Jesus sat down in the boat to teach the crowd. When Jesus had finished speaking, he told Simon, **'Row the boat out into the deep water and let your nets down to catch some fish.'** *'Master,' Simon answered, 'we have worked hard all night long and have not caught a thing. But if you tell me to, I will let the nets down.' They did it and caught so many fish that their nets began ripping apart. Then they signaled for their partners in the other boat to come and help them. The men came, and together they filled the two boats so full that they both began to sink."* [14] Now keep in mind Simon was an experienced fisherman—he did this for a living. So, it would be understandable if he became a bit angry that this "Preacher" was telling him how to do his job. But he did what Jesus said and caught more than he could handle!

Jesus didn't tell him to overhaul what he was doing He just told him to change one thing—*"row the boat out into deep water."* In other words, "Keep doing what you're doing, don't quit, just change **this**." That slight change made the difference between empty nets and a full catch. But what if Simon quit? What if he said, "Master we have worked all night long and have not caught a thing; there's nothing out here. I'm giving up." Look at what he would've missed!!

Another time Jesus helped with their strategy was when He was raised from the dead. He appeared to the disciples while they were fishing in the Sea of Galilee. *"Later, Jesus appeared again to the disciples beside the Sea of Galilee. This is how it happened. Several of the disciples were there— Simon Peter, Thomas (nicknamed the Twin), Nathanael from Cana in Galilee, the sons of Zebedee, and two other disciples. Simon Peter said, 'I'm going fishing.' 'We'll come, too,' they all said. So they went out in the boat,* **but they caught nothing all night**. *At dawn Jesus was standing on the beach, but the disciples couldn't see who He was. He called out,*

*'Fellows, have you caught any fish?' 'No,' they replied. Then He said, **'Throw out your net on the right-hand side of the boat, and you'll get some!'** So they did, and they couldn't haul in the net because there were so many fish in it."* [15] Same thing happened—Jesus told them to change one little thing but what a difference that "little" thing made!!

Persistence is Essential

I believe in the power of persistence because history has proven over and over that those who don't quit win. It may take longer than expected, they may suffer defeat, but in the end victory is theirs. I saw what it did for a widow who received her request from an unjust judge (who didn't fear God or regard man); not because she had money, friends, or even favor but because she had persistence. [16] I believe in its power because I heard about a man who went to his friend in the middle of the night saying, *"let me borrow three loaves of bread. A friend of mine has dropped in, and I don't have a thing for him to eat."* He was told no and given all sorts of excuses: *"Don't bother me! The door is bolted, and my children and I are in bed. I cannot get up to give you something."* But he persisted and got everything he needed because he was **not** *"ashamed to keep on asking."* [17]

I believe in persistence because Jesus said, *"**Keep on asking**, and you will receive what you ask for. **Keep on seeking**, and you will find. **Keep on knocking**, and the door will be opened to you."* [18] I believe because I heard about Abraham who was told he'd be a father of many nations in his old age. And even though it looked impossible he *"against hope believed in hope, that he might become the father of many nations." And "he staggered not at the promise of God through unbelief; but was strong in faith, giving glory to God; and being fully persuaded that, what He had promised, He was able also to perform."* [19] And God blessed him for his faith and persistence. I believe in persistence because I saw what it did for Sarah, who had a son when she was past childbearing age, because *"she believed the One Who made a promise would do what He said."* [20]

After Seventeen Years Persistence Made a Way

I believe in the power of persistence because I witnessed first hand what it did for my wife. I watched as she struggled in this country without a green card, I heard the comments from those who thought she was a fool for not marrying somebody to get it. I witnessed as this woman who overcame insurmountable odds to get her nursing degree and license was forced to baby-sit, clean houses, churches, and anything else because she was "locked" out of the American dream. I heard the stories of the people who conned her out of money with the promise that they could "help." I listened as she told me the story of a particular lawyer who said, "Anyone who tells you that you can get a green card for **under $20,000** is lying." I was there as the nursing license was about to expire, with her having no way of renewing it, but believing that God would somehow make a way.

I listened as she told me the days of despondency, despair, and frustration. But I also witnessed the power of persistence as former president Bill Clinton signed into law, on Dec. 21 2000, the LIFE ACT. [21] This law gave her the ability to apply for lawful permanent residence without leaving the country (without the act she would've had to leave the country, apply overseas, and come back in 10 years). In other words, it gave her the opportunity to become a citizen without marrying someone or having a baby to do it!

This woman who endured seventeen years of being talked about and being looked over; seventeen years of missed opportunities; seventeen years of believing in hope that somehow she would get her green card; finally got it on December 16th, 2003. Going against the notion that she couldn't do it unless she was married and/or pregnant, she dreamed an "impossible" dream, and I'm a witness to that dream's realization. The Guide tested her and now the same people who thought she was an idiot cry, "Bravo! We knew you could do it!" She now stands as a beacon of light to those trapped in the same dungeon. *"Praise be to the God and Father of our Lord Jesus Christ, the Father of compassion and the God of all comfort, who comforts us in all our troubles, so that we can comfort those in any trouble with the comfort we ourselves have received from God."* [22]

Don't You Quit

Thomas Edison, who failed more than 10,000 times trying to invent the light bulb, once said, "I have not failed. I've just found 10,000 ways that won't work." Don't give up—sometimes the greatest successes are right after our greatest failures. What if Tyler Perry decided to give up writing plays the week before he was to perform at House of Blues? What if Barack Obama gave up politics after his crushing defeat to Bobby Rush in 2000? What if Edison gave up after his 9,995[th] attempt to create the light bulb? What if Jack Canfield and Mark Hansen gave up on their book after being rejected for the hundredth time? What if my wife gave up her dream of becoming a US citizen and followed the "advice" of those around her? And what if you decide to give up on the dreams placed in your heart? Put to use the law of persistence and don't give up! **Make changes if you have to but don't you quit!!**

GROUP DISCUSSION QUESTIONS

"Can two walk together, unless they are agreed?" [23]

1. Why is it that nothing great is ever achieved without persistence? Why is it always so hard?
2. What are the benefits of trying a different strategy?
3. Why is failure crucial to success?
4. What in your life, ministry, or business have you given up on?
5. According to Tyler Perry, what did He do to make the Lord bless his play? Is that hampering you?
6. How can you help someone not give up?
7. When should you quit? When shouldn't you quit?

10

LAW OF STEWARDSHIP

The law that states in order to be given more one must prove that they can handle and master less

"His master replied, 'Well done, good and faithful servant! You have been faithful with a few things; I will put you in charge of many things. Come and share your master's happiness.'" [1]

"Show me a man who cannot bother to do little things and I'll show you a man who cannot be trusted to do big things." — Lawrence D. Bell, *Industrialist and founder of Bell Aircraft Corporation*

B efore anyone is entrusted with **big things** they're first tested with **small things**. In fact, God never **starts** anyone off with big things. Why? A few reasons:

1. **He's not wasteful** — After Jesus fed a multitude with a few fish and loaves He told His disciples: *"Gather up the fragments that remain, so that nothing is*

lost." [2] And a great formula for waste is starting a person off with big things when they've not mastered small things. But as one proves themselves He graduates them to the next level—which carries greater responsibility.

2. **He never gives a person more than they can handle**—No one gives a baby steak—they're given milk. Why? The baby would choke on the steak. The Bible says that each steward was given talents *"according to his ability."* [3] God knows the capacity of each individual and gives responsibilities accordingly.

3. **He works with us progressively**—David said, *"The steps of a good man are ordered by the Lord, and He delights in his way."* [4] Not the "leaps" or "bounds" but the steps. God takes His time with us. He's not in a rush. He understands that people develop in different ways and at different times. He takes us from step to step.

Some years ago my niece made pancakes for her younger siblings and myself. She gave everyone a pancake (except me...I got three!). Her youngest brother, my nephew, kept bothering her for more. She turned around and with a glare said, "You want two?! You can't even handle one!" I looked at her, ran out the kitchen, grabbed a pen, wrote what she said down, and said to myself, "That's deep...I'm putting this somewhere!" What she said to her brother is often what God says to those who insist they can handle more—even when they haven't proven themselves in less.

What is a Steward

A steward is defined as:

1. A person who manages another's property or financial affairs; one who administers anything as the agent of another or others.
2. A person who has charge of the household of another, buying or obtaining food, directing the servants, etc. [5]

God owns everything. David said, *"The earth and everything on it belong to the Lord. The world and its people belong to Him."* [6] God Himself said, *"Every animal in the forest belongs to Me, and so do the cattle on a thousand hills. I know all the birds in the mountains, and every wild creature is in My care. If I were hungry, I wouldn't tell you, because I own the world and everything in it."* [7] But even though He owns everything He puts people as stewards over it. In fact, Adam was earth's first steward: *"And the Lord God took the man and put him in the Garden of Eden to tend and guard and keep it."* [8] So, in essence, we humans run everything but own nothing.

There are two requirements of a steward—let's look at each in detail:

1. Profitable

"The first servant reported, 'Master, I invested your money and made ten times the original amount!'" [9]

A steward must be profitable. A profitable servant is earmarked for elevation. Regardless of field a profitable person is a promotable person. It's therefore essential to find ways to be profitable in your company, ministry, and the like. The spotlight of attention shines favorably on the person who can, through their results, show themselves to be assets and disfavorably on those who prove themselves to be liabilities. Whether your profitability is in exceeding quota, reducing costs, increasing efficiency and/or effectiveness, being a consistent problem solver, or getting others to produce better (which is the best value) do this so that you shine. **God blesses profitable stewards.**

A profitable person can produce results in almost any situation even with liability stacked against liability. Profitable people see treasure where others see trash. Knowing how to be profitable <u>is more profitable than the profit itself</u>. If you did it once you can do it again. Are the resources you have to work with small? Good. Learn how to be profitable even if you only have **two fish and five loaves of bread.** Learning how to be profitable with small capital is preparation for larger capital. The resources may change but the outcome will remain the same—perhaps be even better! Regardless of profession you're there to be profitable. No employer hires someone they believe to be a liability, much less promote that person. Any employer who hires somebody is, in essence, purchasing something they believe to be an asset. If you are truly profitable you will increase your influence under your supervisor's eye. Those who aren't profitable will remain a part of the crowd and must learn to take orders from those who are.

David Was Profitable

After Saul David was Israel's next king—there was no disputing that. He was handpicked by God Himself. And even though he was destined to rule multitudes God started him off small. For instance, when he was on the run he became a ruler of outcasts: *"When David escaped from the town of Gath, he went to Adullam Cave. His brothers and the rest of his family found out where he was, and they followed him there. A lot of other people joined him too.* **Some were in trouble, others were angry or in debt,** *and David was soon the leader of four hundred men.*" [10]

When this "army" initially went into battle together... it didn't look too good at first: *"One day some people told David, 'The Philistines keep attacking the town of Keilah and stealing grain from the threshing place.' David asked the Lord, 'Should I attack these Philistines?' 'Yes,' the Lord answered. 'Attack them and rescue Keilah. But David's men said, 'Look, even here in Judah we're afraid of the Philistines. We will be terrified if we try to fight them at Keilah!"* [11] In essence what they were saying was, "Are you crazy?! We're scared of them here and you want us to go where they are?? Are you outta your mind?!"

So David ran back to God (I would too!): *"David asked the Lord about it again. 'Leave right now,' the Lord answered. 'I will give you victory over the Philistines at Keilah.' David and his men went there and fiercely attacked the Philistines. They killed many of them, then led away their cattle, and rescued the people of Keilah."* [12] Even though they had a rough start they managed to win that battle. Under David's leadership this army grew and some became part of a special elite force called **David's Mighty Men.**

David was an awesome leader—his people loved him and were willing to do anything for him. One example is when David was in a stronghold and was thirsty: *"David was then in the stronghold, and the garrison of the Philistines was then at Bethlehem. And David said longingly, 'Oh that someone would give me water to drink from the well of Bethlehem that is by the gate!' Then the three mighty men broke through the camp of the Philistines and drew water out of the well of Bethlehem that was by the gate and took it and brought it to David."* [13] Now it's one thing to get your leader a drink of water; it's another thing to break through an enemy garrison, get some water, and break through it again to get it to your leader! David was profitable—he took less and did more—**a lot more** with it!

2. Faithful

"Moreover it is required in stewards, that a man be found faithful." [14]

A steward must be faithful. The Bible says, *"Most men will proclaim every one his own goodness: but a faithful man who can find?"* [15] In other words, "Everyone says they're faithful, but a truly faithful person is rare." Faithfulness is the surest sign of a good steward—and an essential requirement for promotion. *"The Lord said, 'Who, then, is the faithful and careful servant manager whom his master will put in charge of giving all his other servants their share of food at the right time? How blessed is that servant whom his master finds doing this when he comes! I tell you with certainty, he will put him in charge of all his property.'"* [16] **God blesses faithful stewards.**

No one promotes somebody that can't be trusted. If they're irresponsible in their present position, why give them more responsibility? The Bible says, *"Confidence in an **unfaithful** man in time of trouble is like a broken tooth, and a foot out of joint."* [17] Try eating with a broken tooth and putting pressure on an out-of-joint foot—the pain is almost unbearable! *"Never let go of loyalty and faithfulness. Tie them around your neck; write them on your heart. If you do this, both God and people will be pleased with you."* [18]

Moses Was Faithful

Moses and God shared a special relationship. Moses spent as much time in the Presence of God as he could—and God adored him. When Miriam and Aaron spoke against

Moses behind his back, the Bible says, *"At once the Lord said to Moses, Aaron and Miriam, 'Come out to the Tent of Meeting, all three of you.' So the three of them came out. Then the Lord came down in a pillar of cloud; He stood at the entrance to the Tent and summoned Aaron and Miriam. When both of them stepped forward, He said, 'Listen to My Words: When a prophet of the Lord is among you, I reveal Myself to him in visions, I speak to him in dreams. But this is not true of My servant Moses; he is faithful in all My House. With him I speak Face to face, clearly and not in riddles; he sees the Form of the Lord. Why then were you not afraid to speak against My servant Moses?'"* [19] And immediately Miriam was struck with leprosy; and it took Moses, the one they scorned, to intercede on her behalf. [20]

When Korah led a rebellion against Moses and Aaron, God wasted no time in defending His special servant: *"The earth opened its mouth and swallowed the men, along with their households and all their followers who were standing with them, and everything they owned. So they went down alive into the grave, along with all their belongings. The earth closed over them, and they all vanished from among the people of Israel. All the people around them fled when they heard their screams. 'The earth will swallow us, too!' they cried. Then fire blazed forth from the Lord and burned up the 250 men who were offering incense."* [21] But unfortunately many didn't learn because the *"very next morning the whole community of Israel began muttering again against Moses and Aaron, saying, 'You have killed the Lord's people!' As the community gathered to protest against Moses and Aaron, they turned toward the Tabernacle and saw that the cloud had covered it, and the glorious Presence of the Lord appeared."* [22] God was serious about protecting His faithful one! What happened next?? A plague broke out and *"14,700 people died in that plague, in addition to those who had died in the affair involving Korah."* [23]

107

Moses was so faithful that God *"made His **ways** known unto Moses, [but] His **acts** unto the children of Israel."* [24] To Moses God revealed the deep parts of Himself—like friends revealing their hearts to one another. And so it remains today, to the mature God reveals His ways (the deeper parts of Him) but to the immature He reveals His acts (the beginning parts of Him). When speaking about Moses one writer said, *"his work was an illustration of the truths God would reveal later."* [25] Moses was the illustration of true faithfulness and Christ became the reality.

Moses wasn't perfect but he was faithful. And I believe that faithful people are truly dear to God's Heart. *"Then the Lord said, 'Learn a lesson from this unjust judge. Even he rendered a just decision in the end. So don't you think God will surely give justice to His chosen people who cry out to Him day and night? Will He keep putting them off? I tell you, He will grant justice to them quickly!* ***But when the Son of Man returns, how many will He find on the earth who have faith?"*** [26]

Discover the Champion in You

In 2006 he was named one of the "Ten Most Fascinating People" by Barbara Walters, [27] and was also named the "Most Influential Christian in America." [28] He is the author of two bestselling books and is pastor of Lakewood Church—the largest church in America. His weekly broadcasts reach over seven million viewers and more in over 100 nations around the world. But who would've guessed that this quiet, unassuming man who feels he's not so good with people would reach such prominence? For years he worked behind the scenes, was afraid to speak in public, and never thought of becoming a pastor. And yet now millions listen to him every week, follow his lead, raise their Bibles, and say in unison: "This is my Bible. I am who it says I am. I have what it says I have. I can do what it says I can do…"

He was born Joel Scott Hayley Osteen to John and Doddie Osteen. His father started Lakewood Church on Mother's day in 1959—in a converted feed store. The elder Osteen, who at the time was a southern Baptist, was alienated by his denomination for, what they viewed as, unconventional practices: preaching a message of love and eternal happiness when fire and brimstone were the norm, embracing certain tenets of Pentecostalism, and preaching a "prosperity gospel." [29] The church's membership grew and by the late 1970's it had outgrown the feed store and they built a bigger space.

The younger Osteen, who was studying at Oral Roberts University (ORU), decided to drop out and come back to Houston. On one hand, to help care for his mother, who was diagnosed with terminal cancer in 1981 (she's been completely healed), and on the other hand, to start Lakewood's first TV ministry. The elder Osteen agreed but with one catch: the church would never ask for money. While at ORU the younger Osteen kept thinking of ways the church could serve more people—and with his love of marketing television seemed to be the best answer. He left ORU, came home, and immersed himself in the task of expanding Lakewood's reach.

The Steward Behind the Scenes

Osteen worked diligently behind the scenes expanding his father's ministry. "Victoria (his wife) would kid me because I would spend four hours adjusting a light," Osteen said. "I learned you can't separate the message from the presentation of that message."[30] From adjusting a light to picking the suits that would make his dad look good on camera—everything mattered to Osteen. Under Osteen's leadership the television ministry grew by leaps and bounds. Even though Osteen was serving his father faithfully, he grew frustrated with his father's reluctance for rapid expansion:

"At one point I had arranged for a large number of radio stations to carry our weekly broadcast. I said, 'Daddy, if you'll come down to the studio for maybe an hour a week, we can make all these radio programs.' To my dismay, Daddy responded, 'Joel, I don't want to do that. I'm seventy-five years old, and I'm not looking for anything else to do.' I was so disappointed. I thought, God, *I'm young, and I have all these dreams to touch the world; I have lots of energy; I don't want to do less. I want to do more.*" [31]

Osteen was disappointed but he respected his father's wishes.

The elder Osteen, for years, would try to persuade his son to give a message. The younger would always refuse — he had a fear of public speaking. One Sunday the elder called his son at home and asked, one more time, if he would give a message. The younger said no, hung up the phone, and sat down to eat his dinner. But then something strange happened: "while Victoria and I were eating, Daddy's words kept flitting through my mind, and with no other provocation, I began to have an overwhelming desire to preach. I didn't really understand it at the time, but I knew I had to do something. Keep in mind, I had never prepared a sermon, let alone considered standing up in front of thousands of people to speak. Nevertheless, I called Daddy right back and said. 'Daddy, I've changed my mind. I think I'll do it.'" [32] He hung up the phone, and sat down thinking it was the worst mistake he ever made! On January 17th, 1999 the younger gave his first sermon as his father listened in the hospital. The elder died less than a week later.

From the Background to the Forefront

With the loss of Lakewood's senior pastor many critics predicted the size of the church would shrink, or worse, the church would close down. Osteen continued preaching even though he too wondered if the church would survive. "I didn't even dream about growing or expanding or being on television or anything like that," he said. "First thing I did was cancel the television." [33] That decision was quickly vetoed by his wife! On October 3, 1999 Osteen was offici-ated as Lakewood's new senior pastor. Under his leadership the church's congregation has increased more than fivefold—from 6,000 to 30,000 congregants! In 2005, Osteen moved his church into the former Compaq Center—the arena that was once home to the Houston Rockets and the WNBA Houston Comets. [34] The steward who, for 17 years, stayed behind the scenes to make his father look good, now is one of the most influential and inspirational pastors in the world! In his book, he tells the touching story of the last day he saw his father. His father needed to get to the clinic for dialysis and called his son—it was four in the morning. He stayed the entire day, took care of his father, his father told him how much he loved and appreciated him, Osteen did the same, and he took his father home. During that time he said something that illustrates, in my mind, the heart of a good steward: "I told him, 'Daddy, I'm going to do everything I can to make your life better, to make your life more comfortable, to make you proud of me.'" [35] Those are the wishes of a true steward: to make the lives of their master better, more comfortable, and to make them proud. **God honors good stewards!**

As a good steward, Osteen did everything with excel-lence. He had no idea he'd be Lakewood's future pastor; he just did everything he could to serve his father. He tells the time, years before his father's passing, when the church decided to remodel its platform area. The younger wanted everything to be right for the elder. For months he worked with the architects and designers, had a mock-up made of everything, and spent several weeks working on the lighting. "I was committed to excellence," Osteen said. "Little did I realize that one day I would be the one standing on the same platform, behind the same podium. I didn't realize it then, but I was building my own house. Looking back, I'm glad I put forth the extra effort. I'm glad I gave it everything I had." [36]

You are a steward. Whether you're a good or bad one is your choice. Be a good one. Serve your superiors, be profitable, be faithful, be efficient, do more than expected even if no one is looking. The God Who sees what you do *"in secret will Himself reward you openly."* [37] Who knows? The very platform you're building might be the one you'll stand on! *"If you care for your orchard, you'll enjoy its fruit; if you honor your boss, you'll be honored."* [38]

To Whom Much is Given...

Many people believe the journey ends when they finally get "it." With all the servitude, extra miles, and persistence necessary...when "it" is finally acquired they can rest. But getting "it" is only the beginning—now the task is to maintain "it." Again, it's one thing to attain something it's another thing to maintain it. Great people learn how to maintain. Starting small is a blessing—it teaches you how to do more with less. Also, once you finally get the thing you've been after, you'll appreciate it and handle it better. The entertainment world is put to shame by the efficiency, effectiveness, and relatively low costs of a Tyler Perry project. Below are some of the numbers:

Budget: A "low budget" Hollywood film can be shot for $20 million; a Perry film usually costs no more than $12 million to make

Prep Time: A Hollywood film can take 3-12 months of preparation; a Perry film needs only 8 weeks of preparation

Shoot Time: A big budget Hollywood film is usually shot in 100 days; a Perry film is shot in 30 days

Film Production: A major Hollywood movie can take years to complete; Perry completed two movies in less than seven months

Return on Investment: Usually an investor would hope to receive pennies for every dollar invested; for every $1 invested in a Perry project $2.20 was received. [39] [40]

Perry who, at one point, was so broke that he rounded up loose change to buy a package of 60 cookies for a week's meals knows the value of doing **more with less.** "I can do it efficiently at a fraction of what it costs in Hollywood because there are not 20 executives telling you, 'Move the cup to the left' or 'I don't like the color of her sweater.' These are the kind of notes they do on television shows," says Perry. "I go down, look at everything. I like it. We shoot the show. I don't have all these people trying to justify their jobs." Remember: the small prepares you for the great. **Be a good steward.**

GROUP DISCUSSION QUESTIONS

*"When the Feast of Pentecost came, they **were all together in one place.** Without warning there was a sound like a strong wind, gale force— no one could tell where it came from. It filled the whole building.*

Then, like a wild fire, the Holy Spirit spread through their ranks." [41]

1. What does stewardship mean to you?
2. What are the reasons God never starts anyone off with big things? Why does He bless with small things first?
3. What are the two requirements of a steward? How can you as a good steward meet both requirements?
4. Why was Joel Osteen a good steward? What did he do?
5. What does the small prepare you for? Do you have a personal experience to share?
6. Why is the entertainment world put to shame by a Tyler Perry project?
7. What can you do to be a *better* steward?

11

LAW OF SERVICE

The law that states in order to be greatest of all one must be servant of all

"They came to Capernaum. When He was safe at home, He asked them, 'What were you discussing on the road?' The silence was deafening—they had been arguing with one another over who among them was greatest. He sat down and summoned the twelve. 'So you want first place? Then take the last place. Be the servant of all.'" [1]

"The best way to find yourself is to lose yourself in the service of others."
—Mohandas K Gandhi, *political and spiritual leader*

We said before that everyone wants to be great. And everyone has different definitions of greatness—but the one defining characteristic of true greatness is service. Service is the door that leads to greatness. Jesus said, *"For even the Son of Man came not to be served but to serve others and to give His Life as a ransom for many."* [2] There's no way around it. When it was Aaron's time to die God told Moses *"strip Aaron of his garments, and put them upon Eleazar his son: and Aaron shall be gathered unto his people, and shall die there."* [3] When Moses stripped him of his garments (or his robes of service) he died immediately. What does that mean? I truly believe our lives end when we stop serving others—but they begin the moment we do! A life of service is a life well lived.

Servants Empty Themselves

The Bible says, *"Let the same mind be in you that was in Christ Jesus, who, though He was in the Form of God, did not regard equality with God as something to be exploited,* ***but emptied Himself, taking the form of a slave****, being born in human likeness. And being found in human form, He humbled Himself and became obedient to the point of death. Even death on a cross."* [4] A true servant must be humble. They must be willing to put aside all privileges to serve those who need service. And only with a servants mind and heart can we effectively serve. Christ humbled Himself and took the lowest position and God took Him from the lowest to the highest!

To "empty" one's self is to remove all preconceptions, pride, arrogance, brilliance, and even past information. Servants must be empty before they can be filled. To be "full of" one's self is to know the answer without really assessing the problem. When a good salesperson calls on a prospect one of the first things he or she does is a "fact-finder" analysis. This is a series of questions to uncover the prospect's needs. Only **after** uncovering the prospect's needs can the salesperson truly serve. When a doctor meets with a new patient he or she diagnoses the problem **before** prescribing an answer. A company that continually does research to find out what their customers need are in fact "emptying themselves." They realize that to be effective servants they must empty themselves of old information and fill themselves with new. In fact, to effectively learn anything students must first empty themselves. The worst thing a teacher can hear from an ignorant student is "I know."

We all have to empty ourselves periodically. In order to be productive servants we have to keep finding **better** ways to serve. Jesus would say things like: *"You have heard that it was said to those of old...But I say to you..."* [5] He understood that in order to remain effective changes, periodically, had to be made. A person, ministry, company, or organization that refuses to change with the times to better serve people is, in my opinion, doing a **disservice**.

Good Leaders Empty Themselves

In the1990's IBM, once the world's premier computer company, appeared ready for demise. In 1993 it reported a net loss of $8.1 billion, in addition to net losses in 1991 and 1992. [6] It also was losing market share as companies like Compaq moved in and dethroned it as the largest PC maker. In 1993, with no controls on spending and 100 days before its cash ran out a new CEO was appointed: Lou Gerstner. Many outsiders viewed a turnaround as impossible, even Gerstner had his doubts: "It just looked like it was going into a death spiral. I wasn't convinced it was solvable." [7]

Management was overhauled, controls were put on spending, huge layoffs were administered, and tough management decisions were made during his first two years of tenure. By 1998 IBM recorded revenues of $81.7 billion, and a profit of $6.3 billion. The giant once again became whole and today continues on a steady trail of growth and productivity. His turnaround of IBM became legendary. However during his first few weeks of activity he did everything to empty himself. He knew little about the technology and had to learn on the job. In addition to his hectic schedule his first few weeks were spent analyzing the company and asking questions of staff. He was always seen with a pad and pen taking notes. He emptied himself of any preconceptions and did a thorough analysis of the problem at hand.

When Nehemiah received the go-ahead to rebuild Jerusalem's walls he didn't come in prophesying, giving out orders, or proclaiming victory he simply emptied himself of what he knew and inspected the premises: *"Under cover of night I went past the Valley Gate toward the Dragon's Fountain to the Dung Gate looking over the walls of Jerusalem, which had been broken through and whose gates had been burned up. I then crossed to the Fountain Gate and headed for the King's Pool but there wasn't enough room for the donkey I was riding to get through. So I went up the valley in the dark **continuing my inspection of the wall.** I came back in through the Valley Gate. The local officials had no idea where I'd gone or what I was doing—I hadn't breathed a word to the Jews, priests, nobles, local officials, or anyone else who would be working on the job."* [8]

At the end of his life Paul said, *"I am **already being poured out as a drink offering**, and the time of my departure is at hand. I have fought the good fight, I have finished the race, I have kept the faith. Finally, there is laid up for me the crown of righteousness, which the Lord, the righteous Judge, will give to me on that Day, and not to me only but also to all who have loved His appearing."* [9] Good leaders and/or servants empty themselves.

Service is the Best Form of Marketing

Everybody's marketing for something. Whether it be a ministry marketing for more members, a company marketing for more customers, an organization marketing for more

supporters, a politician marketing for voters, an evange-
list marketing for converts, the unemployed marketing for
employment, and etc. Every day we're swamped with ads
that tell us to "buy this" "trust this" "donate here" "eat this"
"don't eat this" "come to this church" "don't go to that
church" "come see this person speak" and etc. In fact, ad
spending increased from $50 million in 1867 to $22.4 billion
in 1974! [10]

And yet Jesus was so effective in marketing, that with no
marketing budget, no blog, no social media, no ads in televi-
sion, radio, or the internet He drew crowds so huge that most
Chief Marketing Officers would've passed out from disbe-
lief! What did He do?? What was His marketing strategy?
Did He give out flyers? Did He have a mass email campaign?
Newsletters? Did He go up to everybody and say "Hey, buy
My stuff!" Did He spend a lot of money on commercials??
What did He do???

He served. He met needs. The Bible says, *"He used
synagogues for meeting places and taught people the truth
of God. God's kingdom was His theme—that beginning right
now they were under God's government, a good government!* ***He also healed people of their diseases and of the bad
effects of their bad lives. Word got around the entire Roman
province of Syria.*** *People brought anybody with an ailment,
whether mental, emotional, or physical.* ***Jesus healed them,
one and all. More and more people came, the momentum
gathering.*** *Besides those from Galilee, crowds came from
the 'Ten Towns' across the lake, others up from Jerusalem
and Judea, still others from across the Jordan."* [11]

He became so popular that at times He couldn't even
walk in open towns He had to stay in the desert; He was so
popular that when He stayed at a house it *"was so packed
with visitors that there was no more room, even outside
the door."* [12] Could you imagine a marketing campaign so
effective that security would be at the front door telling pros-

pects: "Back! Back! There's no more room! Try tomorrow! We can't fit anybody else! Back!!"

The Bible says, *"If you extend your soul to the hungry and satisfy the afflicted soul, Then your **light shall dawn in the darkness, and your darkness shall be as the noonday."*** [13] In other words if you serve people you'll move from obscurity to notoriety; from mediocrity to greatness. Imagine how effective a marketing strategy could be if it moved from "finding ways to best **get** people" to "finding ways to best **serve** people."

"We'll Pick You Up"

What began in the basement of a St. Louis, Missouri dealership over 50 years ago continues to astound outsiders. While many of its competitors are plagued with decreasing market share, decreased profits, bankruptcy, and other troubles this company has continued on a slow but steady trail of growth and profitability. It's known worldwide for its customer service—and attempts to make every customer "completely satisfied." It believes in going the "extra mile" for customers and rewards those employees that do. This company which is driven by a simple creed: "Take care of your customers and employees first, and profits will follow." But who knew it would reach such prominence? Who could've imagined a company that was under "the radar" for years would one day dominate its industry?

Enterprise Rent-A-Car is the largest rental car company in North America. It has more than 7,000 offices with revenues topping $10 billion in 2008. What's astonishing is not its size, fleet, revenues, or work force but its customer service. The company has a culture of customer service that's been one of the main reasons for its phenomenal growth. Some of the awards for its service are as follows:

- Ranked on **Business Week's** list of "Customer Service Champs" – 2007 and 2008.
- Ranked highest in customer satisfaction by **J.D. Power and Associates** for rental car companies at or near airports 8 out of the last 9 years.
- Repeatedly ranks number one on the **Market Metrix Hospitality Index** in rental car industry customer satisfaction – 23 out of 24 times since MMHI was instituted in 2002.
- Ranks in the **Top 50 Most Respected Companies in the U.S.** in survey of consumers conducted by Reputation Institute. [14]

Humble Beginnings

The company was started in 1957, by Jack Taylor. Taylor, at the time was a sales manager at Lindburg Cadillac. Growing up Taylor didn't consider himself an exceptional student: "I despised Monday mornings more than anything as a kid, because I knew the teacher was going to call on me at school and I wouldn't get the answer right." [15] After graduating from high school he tried college. But, after one semester at Westminster College and another at Washington University he dropped out. He tried to join the military after the Pearl Harbor attack but was rejected because he had hay fever. He tried the navy and was accepted.

He flew F6F Hellcat fighters from the decks of the USS *Essex* and the USS *Enterprise*. By the time he completed his service in 1945 he had received two Distinguished Flying Crosses and the Navy Air Medal. [16] After the Navy he looked into becoming a stockbroker (but decided against it), had brief employment with a local newspaper, and started a delivery service. Arthur Lindburg, owner of Lindburg Cadillac, heard about Taylor and asked through his father if he'd be interested in working for him. Taylor politely turned him down. A few months later Lindburg, in person, asked Taylor again to work for him at a starting salary of $400 a month. This time Taylor agreed.

Taylor started out at Lindburg's dealership doing menial jobs. After a few months he moved on to selling cars and later went on to become sales manager. After a few years Taylor began contemplating his future in car sales; he saw much greater potential in a new concept in the car industry: automobile leasing. So one day he approached his boss with the idea of starting a leasing business; and with seven cars Executive Leasing was born.

From Leasing to Renting

The leasing business was growing steadily but Taylor's customers also inquired about loaner cars. At first he told them 'no' but that had consequences: "Good customers would kind of get mad," Taylor said. "So we'd reluctantly tell them, 'Okay, we'll give you something for these short-term needs.'" [17] In 1962 Executive Leasing added a rental car division. In 1963 Taylor asked Don Holtzman to run the rental car division. [18] At the time, the largest rental car companies were stationed at the airport (for customers who needed a car while on a trip), so they focused on the city.

They found their market by working with insurance adjusters who needed cars for customers whose cars had been stolen or damaged. It was an untapped pool of potential renters. Focusing on the "home-city" market with undeniable customer service the fledgling rental car business grew. In 1969 the business expanded beyond St. Louis and changed its name to "Enterprise." In 1974 it came up with the innovative idea of providing customers with a free ride to the rental office.

Enterprise Service Quality Index (ESQi)

The company continued to grow under the radar and by 1996 became the largest rental car company in America — but there was a problem. "We were growing rapidly back then, and problems were starting to arise," said Andy Taylor (Jack Taylor's son), present CEO and Chairman. "We were doing more business, getting more customers, but we were also getting a lot more complaints from customers." So they decided to add metrics to their customer service. "We created a measurement called ESQi, which is the Enterprise Service Quality index. It's a statistically valid sample of customers' opinions taken monthly, at every one of our branches."

How does it work? First, a customer is called and asked to rate their Enterprise experience. There are five answers that range from "completely satisfied" to "completely dissatisfied." Second, they're asked would they come back to Enterprise. If a customer is "completely satisfied" that's one point — anything less than that is nothing. Beginning in 1996, all employees were told if they weren't at corporate average or above on ESQi, they weren't getting promoted — ESQi quickly improved!Today, the $3.5 million annual cost of ESQi seems like a bargain: "The process enabled us to go from being a nearly $2 billion business in 1994 to a $7 billion plus business (in 2004)," Taylor added. "We lost a few people along the way, but it was the best thing we could have done." [19]

Enterprise Rent-A-Car (or ERAC) truly has a customer service culture that is admirable. Many organizations (ministries or enterprises) would benefit from such a culture. How did they do it? Well here a few of their methods:

- **It starts with the top** — From its inception the company has made customer service a way of life. The philosophy of "take care of your customers and employees first, and profits will follow" has endured over a half a century of changes. Whatever's at the top will trickle down—whether good or bad *"it's like costly anointing oil flowing down head and beard... like the dew on Mount Hermon flowing down the slopes of Zion."* [20] Jesus Himself said, *"Most assuredly, I say to you, the Son can do nothing of Himself, but what He **sees** the Father do; for whatever **He does, the Son also does in like manner."*** [21] In other words, the person **under charge** will only do what the person **in charge** is doing. Even now Andy Taylor calls his father the "minister of culture" because when he speaks to him the inevitable question that comes up is "Andy, are the customers happy?"

* **Train thoroughly**— The bulk of ERAC recruits are fresh college graduates; when hired they go through a rigorous customer service training. And through their careers they are constantly trained and retrained on how to deliver exceptional customer service. From day one the concept of service is deeply ingrained. One time a friend of mine who worked for ERAC got a call on his personal cell phone. He looked at the phone, pressed the "speak" button, and almost unconsciously said, "Thanks for choosing Enterprise this is George speaking, how may I help you?" Talk about good training!!

The Bible says, *"If the ax is dull and its edge unsharpened, more strength is needed but skill will bring success."* [22] We call people who are skilled and/or knowledgeable about a certain topic *sharp*— because with less strength they can typically accomplish much more than others. Enterprise invests considerable time, money, and resources to keep their staff *sharp*. Jesus also spent considerable time with His disciples—He wanted them *sharp*! In fact, He was harder on them (in my opinion) than He was with others. For example, when He was ready to depart Philip asked Him to show them the Father, hear Jesus' response: *"You've been with Me all this time, Philip, and you still don't understand? To see Me is to see the Father. So how can you ask, 'Where is the Father?'"* [23] In other words, "I've been with you for so long and you still don't get it?!"

- **Treat people like owners**—Each Enterprise branch is run by managers who treat the business like their own. Their pay is directly tied to the performance of the branch. As they increase profits through increased business, controlled costs, etc they're rewarded accordingly. Also, it sets them up for promotional opportunities (which also mean more money). This fosters a sense of ownership and unleashes **huge** amounts of creativity and untapped potential. In fact, a manager from Orlando was the one who spearheaded Enterprise's wildly successful "we'll pick you up" campaign. Most of their innovations come from staff—not from the senior management.

Jesus said, *"I am the Good Shepherd. The Good Shepherd lays down His Life for the sheep. He who is a hired hand and not a shepherd, who does not own the sheep, sees the wolf coming and leaves the sheep and flees, and the wolf snatches them and scatters them. He flees because he is a hired hand and cares nothing for the sheep."* [24] A shepherd is vastly different from a hired hand—the shepherd has a sense of ownership while the hired hand doesn't. As a result, when adversity comes the hired hand is gone! Most organizations treat people like **hired hands** instead of like **shepherds**. They hire people with immense potential and creativity and then treat them like "go fors"—"go for this, go for that, and I'll make all the decisions." But when people are treated like shepherds—they're being listened to, they feel like their ideas matter, they're given greater responsibility, they're treated like people instead of numbers on a financial statement, and etc— they'll be willing to give their **all** for the organization. Some will even lay down their *"life for the sheep."*

- **Promote from within and from the ground up**— Most of the senior and middle-level management started as management trainees. Even the present CEO and chairman (the boss's son) started out washing cars! From the beginning they learn and are in involved in **all** aspects of the business. The company promotes from within so even a management trainee has the potential to become a senior manager. When David became king of Israel one of his first tasks was to conquer Jerusalem. The Jebusites who lived there taunted him believing he couldn't get in. So David decided to promote from within: *"David had told his troops, 'The first soldier to kill a Jebusite will become my army commander.' And since Joab son of Zeruiah attacked first, he became commander."* [25] David opened a new position in his organization, interviewed his people, and Joab got the job! People want to be in an organization where there's growth and opportunity for advancement. Nobody wants to be in something that's dead or dying. We're all growth oriented—because anything that's not growing is dying. That's why Jethro was so upset with Moses! He saw Moses doing everything himself and corrected him immediately. His advice was essentially this: "Find people who are competent, promote them, and make sure to promote from the inside!"

Service Has Many Faces

The Bible says, *"There are different kinds of gifts...there are different ways to serve...there are different ways to work."* [26] Dr. King once said, "If you want to be important—wonderful. If you want to be recognized—wonderful. If you want to be great—wonderful. But recognize that he who is greatest among you shall be your servant...by giving that definition of greatness, it means that everybody can be great. Because everybody can serve. You don't have to have a college degree to serve. You don't have to make your subject and your verb agree to serve... You only need a heart full of grace. A soul generated by love." He was absolutely right! Service is not one dimensional—we were all meant to serve in different ways. Everybody has their own definition of greatness but that definition means nothing without service.

Most people believe that to serve means only being in "ministry"—that's not true. God has given us all different talents, abilities, and strengths. People like Abraham, Isaac, Jacob, Joseph, Daniel, and etc weren't in the "ministry" but they served. And God honored them because they honored Him by serving others. Use your gifts, your talents, abilities, and resources and find ways to serve—remember: *"there are different ways to work."*

Last point: you don't have to be "influential" and/or "great" to help others. Anybody can serve. In fact, I believe God honors "lowly" service more than "great" service. One day Jesus sat down and watched people bring in their temple offering. He watched people give in their money—some even gave in **huge amounts**! Then He watched as a poor widow woman put in two small coins. He was so amazed that He called His disciples to show them: *"I tell you the truth, this poor widow gave more than all those rich people. They gave only what they did not need. This woman is very poor, but she*

127

gave all she had; she gave all she had to live on." [27] What she gave was **small** but she gave *"all she had!"* Be a good servant. *"Whenever you possibly can, do good to those who need it. Never tell your neighbors to wait until tomorrow if you can help them now."* [28]

GROUP DISCUSSION QUESTIONS

"I can guarantee again that if two of you agree on anything here on earth, My Father in heaven will accept it. Where two or three have come together in My Name, I am there among them." [29]

1. What does service mean to you?
2. What are the characteristics of a true servant?
3. Why do servants and/or leaders empty themselves? Why do we have to empty ourselves periodically?
4. Why is it a disservice to not make changes to better serve people?
5. Do you believe service is the best form of marketing? Why? Why not?
6. What can organizations and/or ministries learn from Enterprise Rent-A-Car regarding service? Is it applicable?
7. Why does greatness mean nothing without service?

12

GREATNESS REVISITED

"Now the Lord said to Abram, 'Go from your country and your kindred and your father's house to the land that I will show you. And I will make of you a great nation, and I will bless you and make your name great, so that you will be a blessing...and in you all the families of the earth shall be blessed.'" [1]

"Our deepest fear is not that we are inadequate. Our deepest fear is that we are powerful beyond measure. It is our light, not our darkness that most frightens us. We ask ourselves, 'Who am I to be brilliant, gorgeous, talented, fabulous?' Actually, who are you not to be? You are a child of God. Your playing small does not serve the world. There is nothing enlightened about shrinking so that other people won't feel insecure around you. We are all meant to shine, as children do. We were born to make manifest the glory of God that is within us. It's not just in some of us; it's in everyone. And as we let our own light shine, we unconsciously give other people permission to do the same. As we

are liberated from our own fear, our presence automatically liberates others."—Marianne Williamson, *A Return to Love*

One day while walking Jesus was followed by two blind men. These blind men cried out to Him for mercy—they wanted to see. After a brief conversation *"He touched their eyes and said, 'Become what you believe.'"* [2] It is my hope that after reading this, you believe that you were meant to be great and you'll *"become what you believe."* Remember: like Abraham you become great to make others great; you're blessed to be a blessing.

These laws are timeless and timely; they'll work if you work them! How did I learn about them?? I wish I could tell you I learned them just through studying, or through my successes, or that God spoke out of heaven and said, "Write what I tell you to write, saith the Lord!" But if I said that I'd be lying. Truth of the matter is, I learned about these laws through my own failures. I learned about the importance of vision by not having one, the importance of going the extra mile by only going the first, the importance of persistence by giving up too quickly, the importance of stewardship by being a poor one, and the importance of service by not doing enough of it. Sorry I didn't tell you earlier...we were getting to know each other. I feel like I know you a little bit better now...and I hope you can say the same.

The Greatest Man Who Ever Lived

After looking at most of the people whom we consider great— some living and most dead and gone—I have to conclude that Jesus was the greatest Person Who ever lived. He embodies what true greatness is:

- He put to use the **law of vision**—He knew where He came from and where He was going.
- He put to use the **law of the extra mile**—He went many miles to fulfill His purpose; He truly sacrificed Himself to get the job done.
- He put to use the **law of persistence**—He never quit until He finished His mission.
- He put to use the **law of stewardship**—He was profitable and faithful with the resources He was given.
- He put to use the **law of service**—He served others, served His Father, emptied Himself, and was obedient unto death.

He also put to use the greatest of all laws—the **law of love**. This law stands head and shoulders above the rest and He modeled it so that we could practice it. James said it best, *"But if you keep the greatest law of all, as it is given in the Holy Writings, 'Have love for your neighbor as for yourself,' you do well."* [3]

Jesus gave His all for us and in the end God truly raised Him up! Paul said, *"You know the generous grace of our Lord Jesus Christ. Though He was rich, yet for your sakes He became poor, so that by His poverty He could make you rich."* [4] Or as a great theologian once stated, "The Son of God became the Son of Man that the sons of men might become the sons of God." [5]

It's Not About You

As we conclude know that God has a purpose and a plan for your life. He Himself said, *"'For I know the plans I have for you,' declares the Lord, 'plans to prosper you and not to harm you, plans to give you hope and a future.'"* [6] This may be the end of our journey—but not the end of yours. There are seeds of greatness inside of you that need to be cultivated and brought to fruition. Put these laws to use, help someone else achieve their own greatness, teach others what you have learned, and *"become what you believe."*

But know this: the purpose of your greatness is **for His Glory!** It's not about you…it's all about Him! David with all his wealth and influence understood this simple truth: *"King David went in, took his place before God, and prayed: 'Who am I, my Master God, and what is my family, that You have brought me to this place in life?…What can I possibly say in the face of all this? You know me, Master God, just as I am.* ***You've done all this not because of who I am but because of Who You Are*** *—out of Your very Heart! But You've let me in on it.'"* [7] Ultimately, our purpose on earth is to know and serve Him…beyond that nothing else matters! *"After all this, there is only one thing to say: Have reverence for God, and obey His commands,* ***because this is all that we were created for.****"* [8]

> *"Now unto Him that is able to do exceeding abundantly above all that we ask or think,* ***according to the power that worketh in us****, Unto Him be glory in the church by Christ Jesus throughout all ages, world without end. Amen."* [9]

APPENDIX

The Four Spiritual Laws

By Bill Bright

Just as there are physical laws that govern the physical universe, so are there spiritual laws that govern your relationship with God.

LAW 1: *God **loves** you and offers a wonderful **plan** for your life.*

God's Love
"God so loved the world that He gave His one and only Son, that whoever believes in Him shall not perish but have eternal life" (John 3:16, NIV).

God's Plan
[Christ speaking] "I came that they might have life, and might have it abundantly" [that it might be full and meaningful] (John 10:10).

Why is it that most people are not experiencing the abundant life? Because...

LAW 2: *Man is **sinful** and **separated** from God. Therefore, he cannot know and experience God's love and plan for his life.*

Man Is Sinful
"All have sinned and fall short of the glory of God" (Romans 3:23).

Man was created to have fellowship with God; but, because of his own stubborn self-will, he chose to go his own independent way and fellowship with God was broken. This self-will, characterized by an attitude of active rebellion or passive indifference, is an evidence of what the Bible calls sin.

Man Is Separated
"The wages of sin is death" [spiritual separation from God] (Romans 6:23).

This diagram illustrates that God is holy and man is sinful. A great gulf separates the two. The arrows illustrate that man is continually trying to reach God and the abundant life through his own efforts, such as a good life, philosophy, or religion — but he inevitably fails.

The third law explains the only way to bridge this gulf...

LAW 3: *Jesus Christ is God's **only** provision for man's sin. Through Him you can know and experience God's love and plan for your life.*

He Died In Our Place
"God demonstrates His own love toward us, in that while we were yet sinners, Christ died for us" (Romans 5:8).

He Is the Only Way to God
"Jesus said to him, 'I am the way, and the truth, and the life; no one comes to the Father but through Me'" (John 14:6).

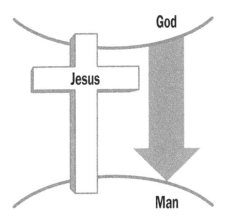

This diagram illustrates that God has bridged the gulf that separates us from Him by sending His Son, Jesus Christ, to die on the cross in our place to pay the penalty for our sins. It is not enough just to know these three laws...

LAW 4: *We must individually **receive** Jesus Christ as Savior and Lord; then we can know and experience God's love and plan for our lives.*

We Must Receive Christ
"As many as received Him, to them He gave the right to become children of God, even to those who believe in His name" (John 1:12).

We Receive Christ Through Faith
"By grace you have been saved through faith; and that not of yourselves, it is the gift of God; not as a result of works that no one should boast" (Ephesians 2:8,9).

When We Receive Christ, We Experience a New Birth
(Read John 3:1–8.)

We Receive Christ Through Personal Invitation
[Christ speaking] "Behold, I stand at the door and knock; if any one hears My voice and opens the door, I will come in to him" (Revelation 3:20).

Receiving Christ involves turning to God from self (repentance) and trusting Christ to come into our lives to forgive our sins and to make us what He wants us to be. Just to agree intellectually that Jesus Christ is the Son of God and that He died on the cross for our sins is not enough. Nor is it enough to have an emotional experience. We receive Jesus Christ by faith, as an act of the will.

These two circles represent two kinds of lives:

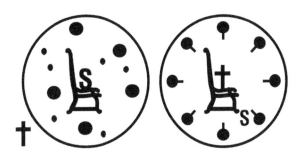

Which circle best represents your life?
Which circle would you like to have represent your life?
The following explains how you can receive Christ:

You Can Receive Christ Right Now by Faith Through Prayer

(Prayer is talking with God)
God knows your heart and is not so concerned with your words as He is with the attitude of your heart. The following is a suggested prayer:

> *Lord Jesus, I need You. Thank You for dying on the cross for my sins. I open the door of my life and receive You as my Savior and Lord. Thank You for forgiving my sins and giving me eternal life. Take control of the throne of my life. Make me the kind of person You want me to be.*

Does this prayer express the desire of your heart?
If it does, I invite you to pray this prayer right now, and Christ will come into your life, as He promised.

How to Know That Christ Is in Your Life

Did you receive Christ into your life? According to His promise in Revelation 3:20, where is Christ right now in relation to you? Christ said that He would come into your life. Would He mislead you? On what authority do you know that God has answered your prayer? (The trustworthiness of God Himself and His Word.)

The Bible Promises Eternal Life to All Who Receive Christ
"God has given us eternal life, and this life is in His Son. He who has the Son has the life; he who does not have the Son of God does not have the life" (1 John 5:11–13).

Thank God often that Christ is in your life and that He will never leave you (Hebrews 13:5). You can know on the basis of His promise that Christ lives in you and that you have eternal life from the very moment you invite Him in. He will not deceive you.

An important reminder…

Do Not Depend on Feelings
The promise of God's Word, the Bible—not our feelings—is our authority. The Christian lives by faith (trust) in the trustworthiness of God Himself and His Word. This train diagram illustrates the relationship among fact (God and His Word), faith (our trust in God and His Word), and feeling (the result of our faith and obedience). (Read John 14:21.)

The train will run with or without the caboose. However, it would be useless to attempt to pull the train by the caboose. In the same way, as Christians we do not depend on feelings or emotions, but we place our faith (trust) in the trustworthiness of God and the promises of His Word.

Now That You Have Received Christ
The moment you received Christ by faith, as an act of the will, many things happened, including the following:
Christ came into your life (Revelation 3:20; Colossians 1:27).
Your sins were forgiven (Colossians 1:14).
You became a child of God (John 1:12).
You received eternal life (John 5:24).
You began the great adventure for which God created you (John 10:10).
Can you think of anything more wonderful that could happen to you than receiving Christ? Would you like to thank God in prayer right now for what He has done for you? By thanking God, you demonstrate your faith.
To enjoy your new life to the fullest...

Suggestions for Christian Growth
Spiritual growth results from trusting Jesus Christ. A life of faith will enable you to trust God increasingly with every detail of your life, and to practice the following:
G   *Go* to God in prayer daily (John 15:7).
R   *Read* God's Word daily (Acts 17:11); begin with the Gospel of John.
O   *Obey* God moment by moment (John 14:21).
W   *Witness* for Christ by your life and words (Matthew 4:19; John 15:8).
T   *Trust* God for every detail of your life (1 Peter 5:7).
H   *Holy Spirit*—allow Him to control and empower your daily life and witness (Galatians 5:16, 17; Acts 1:8; Ephesians 5:18).

Fellowship in a Good Church
God's Word instructs us not to forsake "the assembling of ourselves together" (Hebrews 10:25). If you do not belong to a church, do not wait to be invited. Take the initiative; call

the pastor of a nearby church where Christ is honored and His Word is preached. Start this week, and make plans to attend regularly.

Special Materials Are Available for Christian Growth
If you have come to know Christ personally through this presentation of the gospel or would like further help in getting to know Christ better, two sites are recommended:
www.startingwithGod.com or **www.growinginChrist. com**

If you still have questions, visit:

www.campuscrusade.org

Bibliography

Intro
1. Romans 9:17 (KJV)
2. Marketdata Enterprises. Press Release. http://www.mkt-data-ent.com/pressreleases/Self-Improvement%20Market%20PR%2002-20-2004.doc.
3. Psalm 75:6-7 (NKJV)
4. Acts 17: 28 (KJV)
5. Faber, Riemer. "The Apostle Paul and the Poet: Paul and Aratus." http://spindleworks.com/library/rfaber/aratus.htm
6. Jeremiah 32:27 (KJV)
7. Proverbs 12:19 (GNT)
8. James 2:14 (MSG)
9. James 1:23-24 (ESV)
10. Proverbs 27:17 (MSG)
11. Proverbs 4:18 (KJV)
12. Psalm 119:71 (MSG)

Greatness
1. Luke 9:46-48 (MSG)
2. Philippians 2:3-4 (MSG)
3. Androzzo, Alma Bazel. If I Can Help Somebody. 1945 (Public Domain)
4. Matthew 13:31-32 (NLT)

5. Matthew 25:14-16 (MSG)
6. Matthew 25:26 (MSG)
7. 2 Corinthians 4:7 (NCV)
8. Galatians 5:22-23
9. 1 Peter 3: 3-4 (MSG)
10. Eliason, Todd. "A Highly Effective Leader." Success Jan.2009: 68-69
11. 2 Samuel 5:12 (KJV)
12. 1 Kings 10: 6-9 (MSG)
13. Proverbs 11:24-25 (NKJV)
14. John 12:24-25 (MSG)
15. Jakes, T.D. Church on Fire: Creative Concepts. T.D. Jakes Ministries. VHS
16. Psalm 16:3 (GNT)

Principles

1. Psalm 119:1;34 (NKJV)
2. Genesis 4: 6-7 (NLT)
3. 2 Timothy 2:5 (NASB)
4. Matthew 7:24-27 (NLT)
5. Romans 2:14-15 (MSG)
6. Romans 7:17-21 (AMP)
7. Psalm 19:7-8 (MSG)
8. Covey, Stephen R. Principle- Centered Leadership. New York: Fireside, 1990. p.94.
9. Galatians 3:24 (NRSV)
10. James 1:17 (MSG)
11. Romans 2:6 (KJV)
12. Joshua 5:13-14 (NIV)
13. Ecclesiastes 4:9-12 (CEV)

Isolation

1. 1 Thessalonians 4:3 (KJV)
2. 1 Samuel 16:11 (MSG)
3. Judges 6:15 (MSG)

4. Judges 11:2 (GNT)
5. Judges 11:5-7 (GNT)
6. Genesis 21:17-19
7. Genesis 32: 24-32
8. Exodus 3
9. Luke 15:17
10. Revelation 1:9-11
11. Obama, Barack. "Barack Obama's Victory Speech." Grant Park, Chicago. 4 Nov. 2008. http://elections. nytimes.com/2008/results/president/speeches/obama-victory-speech.html
12. Scharnberg, Kirsten and Kim Barker. "The not-so-simple story of Barack Obama's youth." Chicago Tribune. com 25 Mar. 2007. http://www.chicagotribune.com/ news/politics/obama/chi-070325obama-youth-story-archive,0,3864722.story?page=1
13. Neer, Bob. Barack Obama For Beginners: An Essential Guide. Hanover: For Beginners, 2008. p.9.
14. "Life of Obama's Childhood Friend Takes Drastically Different Path." By Jake Tapper. ABC News. 3 Apr. 2007. http://abcnews. go.com/GMA/Story?id=3045281&page=1
15. Gonyea, Don. "Obama's Loss May Have Aided White House Bid." NPR. 19 Sep. 2007. http://www.npr.org/ templates/story/story.php?storyId=14502364
16. Mendell, David. Obama: From Promise to Power. New York: Harper Collins, 2008. p.242
17. "A&E Biography Barack Obama" 10 Feb 2008. http://video.google. com/videoplay?docid=-3545343528928314588
18. Psalm 118:22 (NIV)
19. 1 Corinthians 1:26-27 (MSG)
20. Matthew 5:13-15 (NLT)
21. Deuteronomy 7:7-8 (MSG)
22. Proverbs 13:20 (GNT)

Desire

1. Isaiah 6:8 (NRSV)
2. Proverbs 16:26 (MSG)
3. Ruth 1:16-18 (NIV)
4. 1 Samuel 17:26 (NKJV)
5. Mark 10:48 (GNT)
6. Mark 10: 49-51 (GWT)
7. Matthew 15:24-27 (CEV)
8. Romans 1:9-11 (MSG)
9. Proverbs 27:7 (NKJV)
10. Acts 17:16 (NKJV)
11. Acts 17:32-34 (NKJV)
12. 1 Timothy 3:1 (NKJV)
13. Though nothing is wrong with seeking greater influence—power should not be sought for power's sake. The purpose of power is to serve and protect the powerless. Power has the ability to corrupt—especially when used for other than service. History is ripe with examples of people who went mad with power. So how do you attain power and keep your sanity? My answer: stick close to God. As one preacher said, "It's impossible to come out of the Presence of God proud." It's only when we keep close to Him can we maintain any kind of balance.
14. 1 Thessalonians 5:11-14 (NIRV)

Character

1. Romans 5:3-4 (NASB)
2. Corinthians 15:58 (NKJV)
3. Warren, Rick. The Purpose Driven Life. Grand Rapids: Zondervan, 2002. p.177.
4. 1 Kings 6:11-13 (MSG)
5. Psalm 30:5 (NKJV)
6. Ecclesiastes 7:20 (NASB)

7. Jakes, T.D. The Ten Commandments of Working in a Hostile Environment. New York: Berkley Books, 2005. p.120
8. 1 Samuel 13:14
9. Proverbs 12:24 (KJV)
10. 1 Samuel 18:5 (ESV)
11. Proverbs 22:29 (NLT)
12. Matthew 9:17 (NLT)
13. "Capacity." Online Etymology Dictionary. Nov 2001. http://www.etymonline.com/index. php?search=capacity&searchmode=none
14. Matthew 5:48 (NLT)
15. 1 Timothy 3:6
16. Ecclesiastes 10:16-17 (MSG)
17. Ecclesiastes 10:5-7 (MSG)
18. 1 Corinthians 13:11 (NCV)
19. Exodus 18:21 (MSG)
20. 1 Samuel 24:16-20 (NIV)
21. Proverbs 11:20 (NLT)
22. Hebrews 10:22-25 (MSG)

Law of Vision

1. Proverbs 29:18 (KJV)
2. Exodus 25:40
3. Genesis 13:14-15 (CEV)
4. Genesis 15:5 (MSG)
5. Habakkuk 2:2-3 (NASB)
6. Canfield, Jack, and Janet Switzer, The Success Principles: How to get from where you are to where you want to be. New York: Harper Collins 2005: 51
7. "Reticular Activating System." Wikipedia. http:// en.wikipedia.org/wiki/Reticular_activating_system
8. Joshua 14:10-12 (NLT)
9. Proverbs 4:26-27 (MSG)
10. Proverbs 11:27 (GNT)

11. Jones, Laurie Beth. Jesus, Life Coach. Nashville: Thomas Nelson Business, 2004. p.2
12. Matthew 5:8 (MSG)
13. Ephesians 5:28-29 (NLT)
14. Numbers 13:32-33 (NKJV)
15. 1 John 3:2 (MSG)
16. Exodus 34:29-35
17. Matthew 6:22 (NASB)
18. Colossians 3:12-14 (NIRV)

Law of The Extra Mile

1. Matthew 5:41 (NKJV)
2. "Matthew." IVP New Testament Commentary. http://www.biblegateway.com/resources/commentaries/index.php?action=getCommentaryText&cid=1&source=1&seq=i.47.5.12
3. Matthew 27:32
4. Matthew 5:43-47 (NLT)
5. Ephesians 6:5-8 (MSG)
6. 2 Corinthians 9:6-9 (ESV)
7. Colossians 3:22-23 (KJV)
8. Kiyosaki, Robert and Sharon Lechter. Before You Quit Your Job. New York: Grand Central Publishing, 2005. p.62.
9. Ruth 2:10-12 (NLT)
10. Ruth 2:15-17 (MSG)
11. Liles, Kevin, and Samantha Marshall. From Intern to President: Make it Happen. New York: Latria, 2005. Pgs 116-118
12. "Holist 05." Black Enterprise. Dec 2005:118
13. Esther 2:21-23 (NLT)
14. Esther 6:1-3 (NLT)
15. Psalm 94:9 (AMP)
16. Proverbs 5: 21 (MSG)
17. Esther 6:4-10 (NLT)

18. "The Q&A Interview—Vince Papale." <u>Out &About Magazine</u>. October 2006. <u>http://www.out-and about.com/ Default.aspx?DN=202,201,199,30,4,2,1,Documents</u>
19. Corbett, Jim. "Notes: Papale's special teams' story; Ravens to get offensive?" 26 Jul. 2006. <u>http://www. usatoday.com/sports/football/nfl/2006-07-26-nfl-report_ x.htm?POE=click-refer</u>
20. Proverbs 14:23 (MSG)
21. Ephesians 4:1-6 (MSG)

Law of Persistence

1. Galatians 6:9 (NLT)
2. Genesis 3:17-19 (CEV)
3. Hill, Napoleon. <u>Think & Grow Rich</u>. New York: Fawcett Books, 1960. Pg 134.
4. Perry, Tyler. "Email Messages From Tyler." 08 Jan. 2009. <u>http://www.tylerperry.com/_Messages/</u>
5. Christian, Margena A. "Becoming Tyler." <u>Ebony</u> Oct. 2008:74; 76.
6. Johnson, Pamela. "Diary of A Brilliant Black Man." <u>Essence</u>. 16 Feb. 2006. <u>http://www.essence.com/news_ entertainment/entertainment/articles/diaryofabrilliant-blackman</u>
7. Hughes,Zondra."HowTylerPerryrosefromhomelessness to a $5 million mansion." <u>Ebony</u> Jan.2004. <u>http://findar-ticles.com/p/articles/mi_m1077/is_3_59/ai_111850312</u>
8. Hira, Nadira. "Diary of a Mad Businessman." <u>Fortune</u>. 14 Feb. 2007. <u>http://money.cnn.com/magazines/fortune/ fortune_archive/2007/02/19/8400222/index.htm</u>
9. This is not to say there is a *literal* "Guide." The Scriptures say nothing about such a Guide...but I do love the analogy that Napoleon Hill gave.
10. Perry, Tyler. "Email Messages From Tyler." 04 Mar. 2009. <u>http://www.tylerperry.com/_Messages/</u>

11. Bowles, Scott. "Tyler Perry Holds On To His Past." USA Today 10 Sep. 2008. http://www.usatoday. com/life/movies/news/2008-09-09-tyler-perry_N.htm

12. "Actor Tyler Perry unveils TV, film studio in Atlanta." Deseret News. 5 Oct. 2008. http://findarticles. com/p/articles/mi_qn4188/is_20081005/ai_n29499430

13. "Tyler Perry." Oprah.com. http://www.oprah. com/article/oprahandfriends/gking/gking_20070214

14. Luke 5:3-7 (CEV)

15. John 21:1-6 (NLT)

16. Luke 18:1-5

17. Luke 11:5-8 (CEV)

18. Matthew 7:7 (NLT)

19. Romans 4:18; 20-21 (KJV)

20. Hebrews 11:11 (MSG)

21. "Obtaining Lawful Permanent Residence Status." National Immigration Law Center. http://74.125.45.132/ search?q=cache:C-mV825nV3oJ:www.nilc.org/ immlawpolicy/obtainlpr/oblpr043.htm+Bill+Clinton+an d+Section+245+i+Provision+of+the+LIFE+Act&hl=en &ct=clnk&cd=6&gl=us

22. 2 Corinthians 1:3-4 (NIV)

23. Amos 3:3 (NKJV)

Law of Stewardship

1. Matthew 25:21 (NIV)

2. John 6:12 (NKJV)

3. Matthew 25:15 (NIV)

4. Psalm 37:23 (NKJV)

5. Dictionary.com. *Dictionary.com Unabridged (v 1.1)*. Random House, Inc. http://dictionary.reference.com/ browse/steward (accessed: January 02, 2009).

6. Psalm 24:1 (CEV)

7. Psalm 50: 10-12 (CEV)

8. Genesis 2:15 (AMP)

9. Luke 19:16 (NLT)
10. 1 Samuel 22:1-2 (CEV)
11. 1 Samuel 23:1-3 (CEV)
12. 1 Samuel 23:4-5 (CEV)
13. 1 Chronicles 11:16-18 (ESV)
14. 1 Corinthians 4:2 (KJV)
15. Proverbs 20:6 (KJV)
16. Luke 12:42-44 (ISV)
17. Proverbs 25:19 (KJV)
18. Proverbs 3:3-4 (GNT)
19. Number 12:4-8 (NIV)
20. Number 12:9-15
21. Number 16:32-35 (NLT)
22. Numbers 16: 41-42 (NLT)
23. Numbers 16:49 (NLT)
24. Psalm 103:7 (KJV)
25. Hebrews 3:5 (NLT)
26. Luke 18:6-8 (NLT)
27. Kwon, Lillian. "Joel Osteen Dubbed 'Most Fascinating.'" The Christian Post. 11 Dec. 2006 http://www.christian-post.com/church/Megachurches/2006/12/joel-osteen-dubbed-most-fascinating-11/index.html
28. "Jan 07: The 50 Most Influential Christians in America." CR Online. http://www.thechurchreport.com/mag_article.php?mid=875&mname=January
29. Mathieu, Jennifer. "Powerhouse." 04 Apr. 2002. http://www.houstonpress.com/2002-04-04/news/power-house/1
30. Greenfeld, Karl Taro. "God Wants Me to Be Rich." Conde Nast Portfolio.com. Aug. 2008. http://www.port-folio.com/executives/features/2008/07/16/Megachurch-Preacher-Joel-Osteen/?refer=email
31. Osteen, Joel. Your Best Life Now: 7 steps to Living at Your Full Potential. New York: Warner Faith, 2004. Pg 198

32. Ibid pg. 215
33. "Osteen Leads Lakewood Church Into New Era." Channel 3000. 19 Nov. 2004. http://www.channel3000. com/entertainment/3932949/detail.html?taf=c3k
34. "America's Largest Church Opens in Former Arena." USA Today.com. 14 Jul. 2005. http://www.usatoday. com/news/nation/2005-07-14-largest-church_x.htm
35. Ibid pg. 248
36. Ibid pg. 295
37. Matthew 6:4 (NKJV)
38. Proverbs 27:18 (MSG)
39. Grover. Ronald. "Hollywood's Hottest Investments." Businessweek. 9 Jul. 2006. http://www.businessweek. com/investor/content/jul2006/pi20060709_564966.htm
40. Christian, Margena A. "Becoming Tyler." Ebony Oct. 2008: 76.
41. Acts 2:1-3 (MSG)

Law of Service

1. Mark 9:33-35 (MSG)
2. Mark 10:45 (NIV)
3. Numbers 20:26 (KJV)
4. Philippians 2:5-8 (NRSV)
5. Matthew 5:21-22 (NKJV)
6. Kanellos, Michael and John Spooner. "IBM's outsider: A look back at Lou." C-Net 1 Feb. 2005. http://74.125.47.132/search?q=cache:rUX8ymzOwvkJ: news.cnet.com/2100-1001-828095.html+Lou+Gerstner &hl=en&ct=clnk&cd=7&gl=us&client=firefox-a
7. DiCarlo, Lisa. "How Lou Gerstner Got IBM to Dance." Forbes. 11 Nov. 2002. http://www.forbes.com/manage-ment/2002/11/11/cx_ld_1112gerstner.html
8. Nehemiah 2:13-16 (MSG)
9. 2 Timothy 4:6-8 (NKJV)

10. Daniel J. Boorstin, <u>The Americans: The Democratic Experience</u>. (New York: Vintage Books, 1974), p.101.
11. Matthew 4:23-25 (MSG)
12. Mark 2:1 (MSG)
13. Isaiah 58:10 (NKJV)
14. "Corporate Fact Sheet." <u>Enterprise Rent-A-Car</u>. Oct. 2008. http://aboutus.enterprise.com/files/2008_corporatefact_sheet.pdf
15. Kazanjian, Kirk. <u>Exceeding Customer Expectations</u>. (New York: Doubleday, 2007), p.8
16. Hansford, John. "A Man on A Mission." <u>Washington University in St. Louis</u>. http://magazine.wustl.edu/Summer03/mywashington.html
17. Ibid p.34
18. "History of Enterprise Rent-A-Car." <u>Car Rental Directory</u>. http://www.carrentaldir.com/history-of-enterprise-rent-a-car.html
19. Powers, Kemp. "Andy Taylor: Enterprise Rent-A-Car." <u>CNN Money.com</u>. 1 Sep. 2004. http://money.cnn.com/magazines/fsb/fsb_archive/2004/09/01/8184670/index.htm
20. Psalm 133:2-3 (MSG)
21. John 5:19 (NKJV)
22. Ecclesiastes 10:10 (NIV)
23. John 14:9 (MSG)
24. John 10:11-13 (ESV)
25. 1 Chronicles 11:6 (CEV)
26. 1 Corinthians 12: 4-6 (NIRV)
27. Mark 12:43-44 (NCV)
28. Proverbs 3:27-28 (GNT)
29. Matthew 18:19-20 (GWT)

Greatness Revisited

1. Genesis 12:1-3 (ESV)
2. Matthew 9:29 (MSG)

3. James 2:8 (BBE)
4. 2 Corinthians 8:9 (NLT)
5. Conner, Kevin. <u>The Foundations of Christian Doctrine</u>. Oregon: City Bible Publishing, 1980. p.281.
6. Jeremiah 29:11 (NIV)
7. 2 Samuel 7:18, 20-21 (MSG)
8. Ecclesiastes 12:13 (GNT)
9. Ephesians 3:20-21 (KJV)

Scripture Translations

Scriptures noted NKJV are taken from THE NEW KING JAMES VERSION. Scripture taken from the New King James Version. Copyright © 1982 by Thomas Nelson, Inc. Used by permission. All rights reserved.

Scriptures noted KJV are taken from THE KING JAMES VERSION.

Scriptures noted GNT are taken from THE GOOD NEWS TRANSLATION. Scripture taken from the Good News Translation - Second Edition, Copyright 1992 by American Bible Society. Used by Permission.

Scriptures noted MSG are taken from THE MESSAGE®. Scripture taken from *The Message*. Copyright 1993, 1994, 1995, 1996, 2000, 2001, 2002. Used by permission of NavPress Publishing Group.

Scriptures noted ESV are taken from THE ENGLISH STANDARD VERSION®. Scripture quotations are from The Holy Bible, English Standard Version®, copyright © 2001 by Crossway Bibles, a publishing ministry of Good News Publishers. Used by permission. All rights reserved.

Permissions

CPSIA information can be obtained
at www.ICGtesting.com
Printed in the USA
BVHW070717010720
582657BV00002B/434

9 781607 918837